BE AN EXPERT SHOT

with rifle, handgun, or shotgun

Clair Rees

Winchester Press

An Imprint of New Century Publishers, Inc.

Printing Code
11   12   13   14   15   16

Library of Congress Cataloging in Publication Data

Rees, Clair F.
  Be an expert shot with rifle, handgun, or shotgun.

  Includes index.
  1. Shooting.   I. Title.   II. Title: Be an expert shot.
GV1174. R435 1984   799.3'1   84–19590
ISBN 0–8329–0358–2

Contents

CHAPTER 1

You Can be an Expert Shot

Almost every shooter would like to become a better shot. The beginner needs a lot of improvement and encouragement, but even experienced riflemen, shotgunners, and handgunners can sharpen their shooting skills with the right techniques.

Everyone can learn to shoot better, and it needn't take years of practice to become an expert. Sure, practice is necessary—but all kinds of practice aren't equally beneficial. If you simply take your rifle or handgun to the nearest gravel pit or shooting range and blaze away, you eventually *may* become a passable marksman. You also can take a new shotgun afield and start trying to hit clay targets thrown from a hand trap. Some scattergunners cut their shooting teeth on wild pheasants, ducks, or other game without any kind of practice.

Maybe most of today's shooters are self-taught, but that's learning the hard way and it takes a lot of time and costly ammunition.

There's an easier, faster method you can use to develop top marksmanship skills. Using the right techniques can greatly shorten the learning time a beginner needs to become a passable shot. These same techniques can carry beginners and experienced shooters alike far beyond the abilities of the average marksman.

If you follow the suggestions in this book, and practice regularly, you should be able to put bullets where you want them at long range, qualify yourself as an expert on the range, and enjoy more successful hunting.

What are the payoffs? Aside from the confidence that comes in knowing you can hit what you shoot at, expert marksmanship is obviously important to the hunter. The ability to drop game cleanly at any reasonable range can spell the difference between success and failure on a costly hunting trip. Being able to place your bullet or shot pattern precisely where you want it also means less wounded game.

Even plinking sessions are a lot more fun when you're a skilled marksman. There's a great deal of satisfaction in being able to call your shots, and the ability to make an empty food or beverage can dance to your command is an ego-pleasing experience. The ability to hit tiny targets—like empty .22 rimfire cartridge cases—consistently can't help but increase your plinking pleasure.

As your shooting skills increase, you may be drawn to formal competition. Metallic game silhouette or more traditional paper-punching sports can prove embarrassing to indifferent marksmen. But when you have confidence in your shooting ability, these games provide an exciting, enjoyable challenge.

Shotgunners also can find organized competition close at hand. Almost every rural or suburban community sports a gun club where you can shoot

You need confidence to hit clay targets with consistency, and good shooters have it.

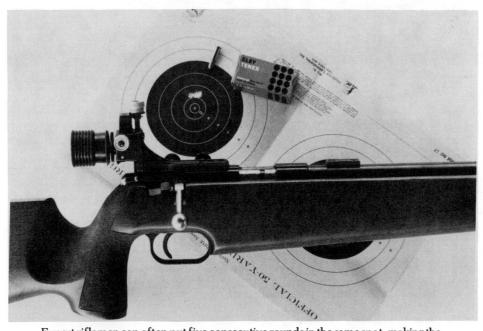

Expert riflemen can often put five consecutive rounds in the same spot, making the target look as if it has just one ragged hole.

skeet or trap. New members are almost always welcome, and the competition is gauged to your own skill. This gives you the chance to win a few trophies from the beginning. Shotgun competition can become a very consuming pastime, and the better you shoot the more you'll enjoy it.

If you're going to shoot *any* firearm—rifle, handgun or shotgun—you owe it to yourself to learn to do it well. Good shooters are safe shooters, and experts are the safest of all. You can't become an expert shot without developing the respect for firearms and gun-handling skills necessary for top safety habits. The shooting expert rarely has an accident with firearms. Safety becomes an automatic, totally reflexive response.

This book is designed as a self-coaching aid. Every attempt has been made to make the instructions as clear as possible, with step-by-step guidelines and illustrations. At the same time, an experienced shooting coach can be helpful. If one offers his (or her) services, don't hesitate to take advantage of them. There are a few exercises listed in which a coach can be particularly useful. These are noted, along with instructions to the coach. In these instances, any

Metallic silhouette shooting is a fun way to sharpen your skills and is one of the fastest-growing and most popular forms of shooting big-bore handguns in the country. The game can also be scaled down to allow rimfire enthusiasts to get in on the action.

helper will do—and you can get along without such assistance, if necessary.

Top marksmanship skills can't be learned overnight, but a single weekend of the right kind of practice can bring noticeable improvement for almost any shooter. Once you've mastered the basics detailed in the following chapters, you'll have the knowledge necessary to achieve expert status. Train your muscles to put that knowledge into practice, and you'll be on your way to new shooting enjoyment.

CHAPTER 2

Rifle Shooting Basics

The first step on the way to becoming an expert rifleman is to learn the basics. Some self-taught shooters never become familiar with the forms and positions that allow the steadiest and most comfortable rifle support. This lack of basic knowledge handicaps them.

Proper breathing and muscle control is easily learned and goes a long way toward improving scores. Ignore these basic skills, and you've placed another stumbling block in your path.

Learning the ten shooting safety rules is even more fundamental. They're based on common sense, and if you follow all ten religiously each time you handle a firearm, you'll never cause a shooting accident. Uninformed shooters who don't know and reflexively follow these rules—called "The Ten Commandments of Gun Safety"—will quickly be ostracized by more knowledgeable sportsmen. No one wants to be in the immediate vicinity of anyone who handles firearms carelessly.

The Ten Commandments of Gun Safety:

1. *Treat every firearm as if it were loaded*. If every rifle, handgun or shotgun you handle is accorded the care and respect due a loaded gun, you'll never have a serious accident. People are killed or injured by "unloaded" guns handled carelessly. Assume *every* firearm is loaded and ready to fire—even if you've checked, and know better.

2. *As soon as you pick up any firearm, immediately open the action and inspect the chamber*. This renders the gun inoperative, and if you've checked to make sure there's no cartridge in the firing chamber there's no way the gun

can accidentally fire. If you're showing or handing the gun to someone else, always open the action first. Leave it open as you hand it to him or her. If someone hands you a firearm with the action opened, you should reaffirm its unloaded condition by inspecting the chamber for ammunition. Every person the gun is handed to should, in turn, visually check the chamber—that's safe gun handling protocol that should always be observed. The action should be left open until the firearm is ready to be returned to its rack or storage area.

If someone hands you a firearm with the action closed, it's proper etiquette to ask him to open it first. If you're about to pick up a gun you're unfamiliar with, ask the owner how to safely open the action.

3. *Always keep the muzzle pointed in a safe direction.* This is actually an extension of the first safety commandment. Since every firearm is to be treated as though it were loaded and ready to fire, it follows that the muzzle should always be pointing in a direction where a bullet or shot charge would do no harm. The muzzle should *never* be allowed to point at a person. At a

Always keep the muzzle of any firearm pointed in a safe direction. When hunting, make sure the business end of your sporting arm is out of harm's way.

shooting range, the barrel should be kept pointing downrange. Otherwise, the muzzle should be pointed at the ground, or nearly vertical at open sky. If you're hunting, keep the barrel pointed away from your companions at all times. This is one rule you should practice until compliance becomes automatic. Watch a properly trained shooter examine a firearm in a roomful of people. The gun's muzzle will be pointed at the ceiling, the floor, or aimed at an imaginary spot on a far wall. But it will never point toward another person.

If you find yourself in the company of someone who handles guns carelessly, you may have the unsettling experience of staring into a muzzle now and then. If this happens, don't hesitate to complain of his carelessness. If he doesn't mend his ways, find a different shooting partner.

4. *Keep guns unloaded when not in use.* Never enter a house or car with a loaded firearm. Guns should be left unloaded until you're preparing to shoot at a target. Transport guns to and from the range or hunting field unloaded and cased. Gun cases protect the finish of your firearms when they're stowed in a car trunk or rattling around with other luggage. Make sure firearms are unloaded when stored at home. As an added precaution, store ammunition separately, and make sure both guns and ammo are safely out of the reach of children.

5. *Be sure the barrel is clear of obstructions*, and that you're using the proper ammunition. Before loading any firearm, first check to see that the bore is clear. Mud, snow, dislodged cleaning patches, wasp nests and other foreign material may plug or obstruct the bore. Firing a bullet or shot charge through even a partially blocked bore can cause the barrel to burst and possibly injure the shooter.

To safely check the bore, first remove all ammunition from the firearm, then open the action. Remove the bolt if the firearm is a bolt-action rifle or shotgun. Otherwise, place a piece of white paper (or your thumb) in front of the bolt to keep the action from closing and to reflect light down the bore. Next, hold the receiver toward a light source and look through the bore from the muzzle end.

When you do get ready to shoot, make sure you're using the kind of ammunition specified by the stamped legend on the firearm's barrel or receiver. Using the wrong ammunition can damage the gun and cause injury to the shooter.

6. *Be sure of your target and backstop.* Know exactly what you're shooting at, and where the bullet will go if you miss before you pull the trigger. Hunters should be absolutely certain they're shooting at game, and not at domestic animals or another hunter. Never shoot at a target on the skyline. If the bullet

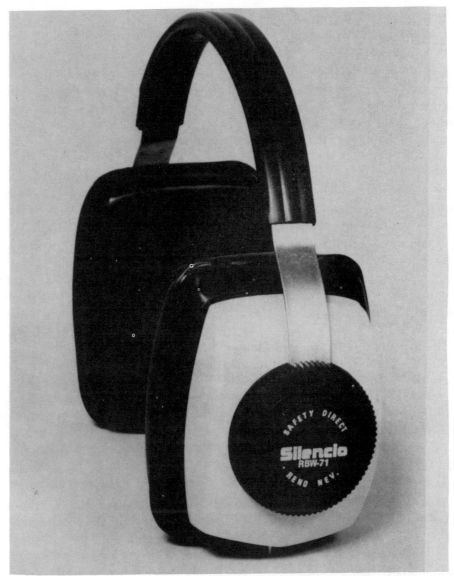

Good ear protectors are absolutely necessary for centerfire shooting practice. Don't leave home without them.

misses, it may travel a mile or more and possibly injure someone out of sight on the far side of the ridge.

When plinking or target shooting, always place your targets against a high, soft bank or hillside. Always shoot into a backstop high enough and wide enough to safely stop stray bullets fired downrange. Never shoot in the direction of buildings, people or livestock. Remember, bullets can ricochet unexpectedly, and someone not directly in the line of fire could be injured if a bullet strays off course.

7. *Never shoot at a flat, hard surface.* Never shoot a rifle or handgun at water. Rifle or pistol bullets can ricochet dangerously when fired at such unyielding surfaces. Bullets can "skip" long distances over water, and in a surprising variety of directions. Even shotgun pellets can spatter back dangerously toward the shooter when they strike a flat, hard surface.

8. *Never climb a tree or fence, or jump a ditch while holding a loaded gun.* When you cross a ditch or fence, always open the action of your gun and make sure no cartridge is in the firing chamber. Leave the action open and hand the gun to a companion until you've safely crossed the obstacle. Then hold your gun and his until he crosses over.

If you're alone, unload the gun, open the action, then slip the gun through the fence several feet away from your crossing point with the muzzle pointing away from you. Don't lean the gun against the fence; lay it down where it can't possibly slip and fall. Make sure you leave the action open. Be sure to keep the muzzle pointing away from you at all times. Never pull a gun toward you by the muzzle.

If you're alone, and you must jump a ditch with your gun, first remove all the ammunition from the chamber and magazine. Then open the action and carry the gun in both hands—muzzle pointing up and away—as you jump.

9. *Never point a gun at anything you don't want to shoot.* Never indulge in horseplay of any kind while holding a gun. Never use the scope sight mounted on your rifle to get a closer look at another hunter or non-game animal. Your firearm should never be pointed at anything you don't intend to shoot.

10. *Alcohol and gunpowder don't mix.* Never drink alcoholic beverages before or during a shooting session. You should also avoid medicines that impair judgement or muscle control when handling firearms. Hunters should leave alcohol alone until the guns are unloaded and safely cased at the end of the day.

If you're unfamiliar with the operation of your rifle, the time to correct that problem is before you head for the shooting range. Most new rifles come equipped with an instruction manual; take the time to read and study this before you attempt to load or shoot the firearm. Make sure you know how the safety operates and how the action functions.

Another basic that should be taken care of before you begin shooting at targets is to see that your rifle is properly sighted in. A surprising number of shooters neglect to make sure their sights are properly adjusted, and that their rifles "shoot where they're pointed." Other riflemen have their scopes "boresighted" by the gunsmith who installed the telescopic sight, and feel this is sufficient adjustment. Boresighting does not guarantee accuracy—it's simply the first step in the sighting-in process. Chapter 5 provides a fast, easy guide to sighting in.

If you'll be doing your initial shooting at an established rifle range there should be shooting benches and sandbags available. If not, take a rolled-up sleeping bag, several blankets, or something else you can use as a rifle rest. An old blanket or tarp will help keep your clothes clean as you shoot from the prone (lying down) position. Be sure to bring along a supply of ammunition, several printed targets (available in any sporting goods store), an empty cardboard box to serve as a target rest if no target frames are available at the range, and either masking tape or thumbtacks to fasten the targets to the box.

If you're a beginning shooter, I strongly advise you to start out with a .22 rimfire rifle. Rimfires are quiet, recoil-free, and inexpensive to shoot. You'll learn the basics of marksmanship much faster without the twin distractions of muzzle blast and recoil.

If you're already an experienced shooter, a rimfire .22 still makes sense for most practice sessions. But if you insist on using a centerfire rifle at this point, you'll need one other item: a good set of muff-type hearing protectors. The report from most centerfire rifles is sharp enough to cause permanent hearing damage, and is almost guaranteed to contribute to flinching. Ear protectors allow you to shoot tighter groups. Interestingly, reducing the noise level of muzzle blast reaching your ears also has the psychological effect of reducing apparent recoil.

The first thing you need to concentrate on is proper sight alignment. This isn't much of a problem with the magnifying scope sights so popular today. You simply place the crosshairs where you want the bullet to go, and keep them steady on target as you squeeze the trigger. You *do* need to keep the vertical crosshair straight up and down. If the crosshairs are canted to one side, the bullet will strike the target low and to one side of the aiming point.

With the open iron sights supplied on some rifles, you have three separate sighting elements to contend with: the rear sight, the front sight, and the target. To aim with open sights, place your cheek snugly against the upper ridge of your rifle's buttstock (called the "comb") and look through the V- or U-shaped notch of the rear sight. Elevate or lower the barrel slightly until the top portion of the front sight blade can be seen. Then further adjust the sight picture until the front sight blade is centered in the rear sighting notch, and the very top part of the front sight appears flush with the top surfaces of the rear sight on either side of the notch.

While maintaining this front sight-rear sight alignment, move the rifle until the front sight covers the target or sits just under it. Most target shooters like to see the bullseye, or the target's center just above the front sight post. When the bullseye appears to sit atop the front sight in this manner, you're employing what's known as a "6-o'clock hold."

Open sights are adequate for relatively short-range shooting, but they handicap the rifleman for long-distance work. The fact that open sights require the eye to try to keep three separate sighting elements simultaneously in focus also presents a problem. Young eyes usually manage to change focus rapidly enough to keep all three elements in register, but this trick becomes increasingly difficult with age.

Receiver sights, or "peep" sights were once highly popular and are still found on most target rifles. To use this kind of sight, you simply look through the rear aperture or "peep," and place the front sight on or immediately under the target. You needn't concentrate on the rear sight at all; in fact it should appear as an indistinct blur. Your eye will automatically center the front sight at the strongest point of light, which falls at the exact center of the rear aperture.

Target shooters use relatively small apertures, but for hunting or field use a much larger aperture is faster and more convenient. Many hunters simply

The prone position is the steadiest and offers the greatest opportunity for accuracy. Notice this shooter's form.

unscrew and remove the rear sighting disc, then sight through the threaded opening used to hold the discs in place. Good hunting accuracy is possible with such oversized apertures.

Once you're familiar with your sights and the proper sight picture, it's time to refine your breathing and trigger control. This should be practiced while you're in the prone position with the rifle steadied by an artificial rest.

Place a target 50 paces downrange, making sure you have an adequate backstop. A printed paper target with a small 2- to 3-inch bullseye works best, or you can simply ink a 2-inch circle on a piece of white paper. Attach the target to a cardboard box or other holder with masking tape or thumbtacks.

Return to the firing line and spread a small tarp or old blanket out to lie on (unless you don't mind getting your clothes dirty). Place a rolled-up sleeping bag or some other soft rest at the front of the tarp.

Assume the prone position by lying on your stomach at a slight angle to the target. Right-handed shooters should lie on a line with their head pointing to 2 o'clock on an imaginary clock face where the target is at the 12 o'clock position. Once you're down, spread your legs a comfortable distance apart and turn the instep of each foot toward the ground.

Grasp the rifle's forend with the left, or non-shooting hand, then allow the forend to rest on the rolled-up sleeping bag. Grasp the pistol grip of the buttstock with your other hand, and allow that elbow to rest on the ground to one side. Pull the buttstock firmly into your shoulder and snug your cheek against the comb of the stock. The butt should be resting in the hollow formed by the juncture of your shooting arm and your upper chest—*not* on the muscle of your upper arm.

Next, adjust your position so the rifle's sights come into proper alignment with the target downrange, and stay there. Adjust the sleeping bag (or other soft rest) until you can keep the sights on target with little or no effort on your part. The rifle should still be unloaded at this point.

While maintaining the sights on target, place the index finger of the shooting hand on the trigger. Only the pad forward of the first joint should contact the trigger. A common mistake is to allow the trigger to rest against the first joint. This area of the finger lacks the sensitivity needed for proper trigger control.

Make sure the chamber is empty and the rifle is cocked. Disengage the safety.

Now keep the sights in careful, continuous alignment with the target, and take a moderately deep breath. Apply a very slight amount of pressure to the trigger, then exhale approximately half the air you've taken in. Hold the remainder of your breath while slowly *s-q-u-e-e-z-i-n-g* the trigger with the front pad of your index finger.

Don't hurry. If the trigger doesn't snap by the time you feel you need to breathe again, relax part of the pressure on it and take another breath or two. Don't resume squeezing the trigger until you've again exhaled half a breath and the sights are steady on target.

When the trigger finally does release it should come as a surprise. If you find yourself anticipating the trigger break, you're likely to flinch slightly or do something else to move the sights momentarily off target. If the sights don't move, but remain steady on target when the trigger breaks, you're doing everything right.

If you have a partner acting as a coach, have him watch the muzzle of your rifle and tell you if it moves or slightly jerks when the trigger breaks. There should be no movement when the trigger releases the rifle's striker or hammer mechanism.

Don't underestimate the importance of this simple exercise. Without proper breathing and trigger control, there's no way you'll ever be an expert marksman. This is fundamental to rifle accuracy.

Once you feel you've mastered breathing, trigger control, and steady sight alignment it's time to repeat the exercise with the rifle loaded. If your sights aren't properly adjusted at this point, refer to Chapter 5. Your rifle should be sighted in before you continue. If you're shooting a centerfire rifle, be sure to wear the muff-type hearing protectors mentioned earlier.

If your rifle has been properly sighted in and you repeat the exercise successfully, a hole should appear in the target very near your aiming point. Three consecutive shots should form a tight triangle, or even make one ragged hole.

After you've fired several rounds, allow your coach to load your rifle while you look away. He (or she) should surprise you now and then by leaving the chamber empty. If the muzzle jerks as the firing pin falls on the empty chamber, you'll immediately know you're flinching. Continue the exercise while your coach randomly loads or unloads your rifle's chamber. Repeat until you no longer flinch when the rifle is left empty.

If you're using a centerfire hunting rifle with noticeable recoil, it's best to confine this exercise to 20 rounds or less. Continuous firing will promote additional flinching and be counter-productive. Postpone repetitions until the next shooting session.

Whether you use a soft-spoken, essentially recoil-free .22 rimfire or a hard-kicking centerfire, this exercise should be repeated at least once every time you go to the firing range. The skills it teaches are best mastered through repetition. Even expert marksmen refresh their memories with this exercise every now and then. It keeps them from developing bad habits through overconfidence or sheer laziness.

While this exercise should be first mastered with a rest of some kind, it can and should be repeated from the unsupported prone, sitting, kneeling, and standing positions.

The unsupported prone position is similar to the supported (artificial rest) position used at the beginning of the trigger and breathing control exercise. The only difference is that no rolled-up sleeping bag or other rest is used. Instead, the elbow of the non-shooting arm, (the arm that supports the rifle's forend) is moved directly under the rifle and used for support.

The prone position is the steadiest of the four basic positions. Its disadvantages are that it takes a few extra seconds to assume, and tall grass or undergrowth can hide the target. Prolonged shooting from the position can be hard on the elbows. Competitive shooters often wear special jackets with padded elbows or use slip-on elbow pads for protection.

The sitting position is faster and easier to assume than the prone position and it's far more comfortable. It also places the rifle and sights on a higher plane where undergrowth is less likely to interfere with the sight picture.

To assume the sitting position, face slightly off-center from the target

The sitting position is easy to assume and offers both comfort and accuracy. Note that the elbows are placed ahead of the kneecaps, not on top of them.

(right-handed shooters should face approximately 2 o'clock with the target positioned at 12 o'clock). Spread your legs a comfortable distance apart, bend your knees and sit down. Keeping your knees well bent, hold your rifle in shooting position. Rest the lower part of each upper arm (just above the elbow) on your legs just forward of each knee. Don't place the elbow directly on the kneecap, as this is both uncomfortable and unsteady.

By scissoring your knees close together, you can raise the point of aim, and vice-versa. The elbow supporting the rifle's forend should be as nearly as possible directly under the forend for the steadiest hold.

The kneeling position is a little less comfortable and not quite as steady as sitting, but many riflemen use it. Right-handed shooters should again face 2 o'clock (southpaws face 10 o'clock). Kneel on your right (left, for southpaws) knee, and extend your other leg until the lower part of the leg is nearly vertical. Sit on your right foot, which can be turned inward or supported vertically by your bent toes. Hold the left elbow directly under the rifle's forearm, and lean forward until the elbow is just forward of the left knee. The knee should support the arm just behind the elbow.

The standing or offhand position is the least steady of the basic shooting stances, but it's the fastest and easiest to assume.

A right-handed rifleman should face away from the target at right angles, or approximately toward 3 o'clock. The rifle is raised to shooting position, while the head turns to face the target. The left elbow should be directly under the rifle's forend. The hand can be positioned at the point along the forend that provides the most comfort. The forend can be supported by the open palm or atop your spread fingertips.

The right hand should firmly grasp the pistol grip, while pulling the butt into the shoulder. The elbow should be held straight out, with the right forearm and upper arm approximately parallel with the ground. Don't slouch—stand as straight as possible.

A rifle sling or carrying strap can make any of the shooting positions steadier. Serious competitors often use the relatively complicated military sling with its multiple loops and adjustable claw-type fasteners. Today, few sportsmen bother with the true military sling because they prefer the greater speed and simplicity of the "hasty sling," which can be achieved with a simple carrying strap.

First, adjust the length of the strap so it's long enough to allow the elbow and forearm of the left (supporting) arm to be inserted between sling and rifle stock. The strap should be twisted a half-turn to the left, then the left arm inserted downward between strap and rifle. Move the strap well up under the upper arm, then wrap the hand and forearm up and around to capture the

The offhand or standing position is fast and quick, but is the least steady of the basic shooting stances.

upper part of the strap tightly behind the left hand as it grasps the rifle's forend. When the strap is properly adjusted, it will run under the knuckles of the left hand, around the wrist, back over the upper arm bicep, and around behind the upper arm to the keeper at the toe (butt end) of the stock. Again, it should be tight enough to create steadying pressure.

Either support-style can be adjusted to accommodate all four basic shooting stances: prone, sitting, kneeling, or standing. Used properly, a rifle sling or

In the offhand position, the right, or shooting arm, should be approximately parallel to the ground.

carrying strap can be a significant aid to marksmanship, particularly at extended range. Unfortunately, many self-taught riflemen regard rifle slings simply as accessories to make carrying the rifle easier. A few minutes practice learning how to shoot while steadying your rifle with a sling are well worthwhile. The skill you gain can be invaluable in hunting as well as on the target range.

Whenever you practice shooting your rifle, be sure to spend some time in all

A full military sling features a loop snugly fitted against the shooter's biceps. While it's a great shooting aid, not too many hunters fuss with it.

four of the basic positions. Repeat the breathing and trigger-control exercises.

You'll find it much harder to keep the sights on target when shooting from the standing and kneeling positions. Typically, the sights will swing back and forth across the target, particularly when you're firing offhand. The trick is to keep that back-and-forth arc as short as possible, and resist the urge to jerk the trigger when the sights swing toward the target. Instead, you should practice taking that breath, letting it part-way out, and *s-q-u-e-e-z-i-n-g* the trigger. Partially release trigger pressure as the sights swing away, and resume squeezing every time the target appears centered in the sights. Again, you should be surprised when the rifle fires. Have your coach watch the muzzle to make sure you're not flinching when the striker falls on an empty chamber. If you flinch or jerk when the rifle doesn't fire, it's obvious you're flinching when it does. If you flinch, you'll miss the target. If you hold the right sight picture while you carefully squeeze the trigger—and train yourself to not flinch—you'll hit what you're shooting at . . . every time.

If you don't have a coach, you can rig a handy aid to help you tell when you're flinching. Simply tie a piece of string to your rifle's muzzle, and attach a

Tying a bolt or some other weight to your rifle's muzzle with a length of cord will help you detect flinching when you practice dry firing. If the object moves, you flinched.

threaded bolt, nut, or some other small weight to the other end of the string 4 or 5 inches below the muzzle. If you jerk the trigger or flinch when the hammer falls on an empty chamber, the weight will jump. If the weight remains immobile as you sight on target and squeeze the trigger, you're doing things right.

Don't be discouraged if you have difficulty hitting the mark from the standing or kneeling position. Everyone has this problem at first. Simply keep on trying. If your bullets stray too far off course from the steadier sitting and prone positions, repeat the exercises from prone while using a rolled-up sleeping bag or some other rest. Master these basics, and you'll be well on your way to becoming an expert.

CHAPTER 3

Choosing the Right Equipment

To be an expert shot, you need equipment that will help you perform at your best. This means an accurate rifle, good sights, and ammunition that shoots well. Good hearing protection is also required.

Other accessories that can be useful include shooting glasses, spotting scopes, sandbags, and adjustable sandbag pedestals. Rifle slings or carrying straps are important, and cleaning gear is a must.

Unfortunately, all rifles aren't capable of top accuracy. Some rifle types are inherently more accurate than others. Bedding, or the way wood and metal meet inside the stock, plays an important part in a rifle's ability to shoot consecutive bullets close to the same point of aim. Some rifles are more critical than others in this respect; the point of impact can change drastically as the wooden stock absorbs or loses moisture. If there are serious bedding problems the rifle will "walk" bullets across the target as the barrel heats and expands.

Rifle sights are also important. Relatively coarse iron sights make fine precision difficult at anything other than short range. Acceptable hunting accuracy is possible out to 150 or maybe 200 yards with open sights, but at that distance the front sight bead obscures much of the target area. Flat-topped front sights are used with the "6-o'clock" hold to give good accuracy on

Of all the types of iron sights available, receiver-mounted aperture sights work best. The eye naturally centers the front sight in the rear aperture, which makes for both speed and accuracy.

printed bullseyes; a micrometer-adjustable rear aperture sight is usually matched with a flat-topped front sight on the target range.

If you must use iron sights, receiver-mounted aperture sights work best. The aperture sight is closer to the eye than the V-notched blade of an open sight, providing a longer sighting plane. Also, the eye doesn't focus on the rear-mounted aperture, making the see-through sight easier to use.

Magnifying scopes are by far the most popular kind of rifle sights in use today. These are available in fixed-power models ranging from 2X upwards, and variable-magnification types in 1½-4½X, 2-7X, 3-9X, 4-12X and other variations.

Riflescopes let you see the target and sight reticle in the same plane. They also make the most efficient use of available light, which gives hunters an edge early and late in the day. The crosshairs are so fine that they obscure little of the target and you can place your shots with precision. The use of a magnifying scope also lets you see the target clearly, providing a crisp, highly detailed image.

Scope-sighted rifles are easy to sight in accurately. Windage and elevation adjustments are clearly marked, and the adjusting screws often have audible-click increments. Quality riflescopes are fog and waterproof, and hold up very well throughout years of hard use afield. They're extremely dependable.

There are several different grades of riflescopes on the market with prices

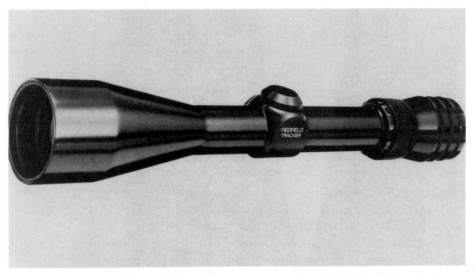

Riflescopes are very popular and allow you to see target and sight reticle in the same plane. Scopes make efficient use of available light, which is very important in many hunting situations.

You should buy the best scope you can afford. This German-made Zeiss is expensive, but offers top quality.

to match. Generally speaking, you should purchase the best-quality scope you can afford. With optical gear, you pretty much get what you pay for. Some of the low-end economy-priced riflescopes simply aren't rugged enough to stand up under heavy recoil or the rigors of hunting. An inexpensive scope may not hold its zero, and will almost always provide an inferior optical picture. It makes little sense to buy a relatively expensive, highly accurate rifle and then economize by buying an inferior scope.

When buying a rifle, you should consider what it will be used for before making your selection. Obviously, competitive target shooting requires a fairly specialized rifle designed for the sport. There are both centerfire and rimfire target rifles, with specialized models intended for metallic silhouette, bench rest, long-range and short-range competition. The National Rifle Association lists rules and rifle specifications for the various target games it sponsors, and there are European-style matches also held throughout the country. Most shooters investing in a rifle strictly for target competition will have a pretty good idea of what he or she needs before making the purchase.

For the hunting or plinking sportsman, the rifle requirements are less stringently defined, and the selection is a lot wider. Deer hunters can choose from bolt-action, lever-action, falling-block and break-open single shots, slide-action and autoloading rifles and carbines. For hunting deer-sized game, any of these models can be relied on to do the job at typical ranges. But beyond 200 yards, certain rifles simply won't deliver the accuracy needed for precise shot placement. Some carbines won't group 3 consecutive shots inside a 3-inch circle at 100 yards, which means you can have your sights precisely "on target," yet still miss your aiming point by 6 inches or more at 200 yards. At 300 yards, you can miss by more than 9 inches even if you do everything right.

This means that some rifles capable of doing an acceptable job in the deer woods at moderate ranges aren't well suited to hunting in the desert or other situations where much longer shots may be called for. A deer may look like a large target, but the vital heart-lung area you must hit for a clean kill is downright tiny by comparison.

Varmint shooters have an even tougher proposition. They may be trying to hit a target area only 2 or 3 inches square at ranges out to 400 yards or more. A ground squirrel or prairie dog looks awfully small at that distance, even when viewed through a 12X scope. Rifles used for long-range varmint shooting must be capable of superb accuracy. Most varmint shooters won't be satisfied unless their scoped, heavy-barreled rifles will deliver minute-of-angle groups or better. A minute-of-angle group is three or more shots fired at a target 100 yards distant, that make three holes measuring an even inch across. The groups are measured between the centers of the two holes farthest apart in the target.

The bolt-action has the best reputation for accuracy of all rifle actions. It's a favorite with big-game hunters worldwide.

Of the five basic rifle action types, the bolt-action rifle has the reputation of being the most accurate. Bolt actions are very strong and stiff, and the simplicity of the tubular receiver design makes positive bedding relatively easy to achieve. Mauser-inspired bolts with front-locking lugs are particularly noted for the unyielding support they give the cartridge case head when in battery. Because bolt-action rifles solidly grip the case head and offer great camming power, they extract even recalcitrant cases from the chamber with great reliability.

As a result, bolt-action rifles are the first choice of target shooters and accuracy-minded hunters alike. Most heavy-barreled varmint rifles are bolt-action models, although there are some excellent single-shot designs that also are capable of fine performance. For overall accuracy, single-shots get the second nod and tend to be less forgiving about bedding and ammunition than bolt rifles are. If you get a single-shot centerfire that doesn't shoot well out of the box, it's often more difficult to get that rifle properly tuned. This is because

Lever-action rifles offer fine "deer woods" accuracy, but aren't the best choice for long-range situations. Don't let anybody put down your "cowboy gun," however. The old standby has accounted for tons of venison in the freezer over the years.

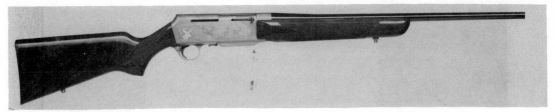

Autoloading rifles like the Browning BAR offer rapid repeat shots and good medium-range hunting accuracy.

the bedding is more critical with most single-shot designs. Bolt rifle accuracy problems are usually more straightforward and more easily solved.

Lever, autoloading, and slide-action rifles aren't noted for top accuracy, particularly for shooting at small targets several hundred yards distant. That doesn't mean you shouldn't consider hunting rifles of these types. All three repeaters will deliver satisfactory accuracy for deer woods use. Most whitetails for instance are shot well this side of 100 yards, and if you don't anticipate any barrel-stretching ranges, a lever, auto, or pump should be perfectly satisfactory. Just be aware of their limitations before you buy.

While the same general comments apply to .22 rimfire rifles, there are several lever, autoloading, and slide-action models that give perfectly acceptable plinking accuracy. Bedding is less critical in relatively low-powered rimfire designs, and unless you intend to participate in formal target competition a lever-action, slide-action, or autoloading .22 should work fine. For some kinds of exhibition shooting, these fast-firing models are actually preferable to bolt rifles and single shots.

If you own a bolt-action centerfire that you feel isn't performing to its potential, there are some remedies you can try. The first (and easiest) is to shoot the rifle from a steady, sandbagged rest to remove as much human error as possible, and try several different ammunition brands and bullet weights. This can prove beneficial with lever, slide-action, autoloaders, and single shots as well. Some rifles exhibit a marked preference for certain brands and bullet weights. If you find a combination that outperforms other ammo types,

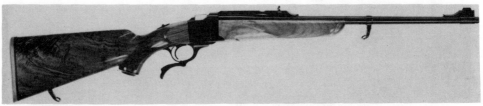

Single-shot centerfires like this Ruger No. 1 are capable of fine accuracy, although bedding is more critical to the gun's performance than with bolt-actions.

stick with it. Using the right ammunition can make a surprising difference in the way your pet rifle shoots.

If you handload (see chapter 23), you can almost always tailor a load that will make your rifle shoot better. This may require some lengthy experimentation, but the results can be well worth the trouble.

If your rifle isn't shooting well, you may be able to correct the problem by simply tightening a few screws. Check the tension on the bedding screws located fore and aft on the action floorplate. If the screws aren't tight, snug them up, tensioning the front screw first. If the screws aren't holding the action firmly in the stock, the rifle can't shoot well.

Check to make sure your scope is firmly mounted. Are the screws that fasten the mounts to the receiver tight? If not, dip the threads in Loc-Tite and re-tension them. Check the screws that fasten the scope rings and give them the same treatment if any are loose.

If the rifle is performing erratically, you might have a problem with your scope. This can be checked by temporarily replacing the scope with another, and shooting from sandbags. If the rifle shoots more accurately with the new scope, send the old one to the factory for repair or buy a quality replacement.

If these steps don't bring improvement, you probably have a bedding problem. If the rifle "walks" shots away from the point of aim as the barrel heats up, there may be a pressure point within the stock's barrel channel. Rub carbon or lampblack along the lower half of the barrel, then replace the barreled action in the stock and snug down the action screws. Disassemble the barreled action from the stock once again, and carefully examine the barrel channel. Pay particular attention to the forward part of the forend. Pressure contact points should be indicated by blackened deposits. Be aware that many bolt rifles are made with a pressure point purposely left about 1½ inches back from the forend tip. If this is the case, it should show even contact.

You can use sandpaper wrapped around a circular block sized to fit the barrel channel to remove stray contact points. Don't overdo things, though. A barrel channel that's too wide reduces the attractiveness of a rifle. After you've removed a little wood, reassemble the rifle and shoot it again.

Some rifles seem to shoot better with some sort of contact between wood and barrel, usually about 1½ inches or so rearward of the forend tip. You can experiment with this theory by inserting small strips of cardboard in the barrel channel at this point. Strips cut from business cards work fine. Again, reassemble the rifle periodically and shoot a few more groups. Varying the tension on the forward action screw can also have an effect on accuracy.

Another tactic that can have positive results is to glass bed the action—or more specifically, the front recoil lug and maybe the first inch or so of barrel channel. This is a job you can do yourself, but if you're not confident of your ability any competent gunsmith can do it for you. A certain amount of wood must first be removed from the inside of the stock to accommodate the fiberglass resin, and the fiberglass should be applied sparingly. Don't forget to thoroughly coat the barrel and action with a release agent first. Glass bedding kits are available at most sporting goods stores. Carefully follow the instructions supplied.

Worn rifling can also contribute to poor accuracy. If the rifling immediately forward of the rifle's chamber appears less than distinct, the throat is worn. Similarly, wear or damage to the rifling near the muzzle can be a tipoff to bad performance.

For best accuracy, rifles should be kept clean and in good condition. Lead and copper fouling should not be allowed to accumulate in the bore. Some smallbore varmint rifles lose the fine edge of accuracy in a hurry if the bore isn't kept clean. Many target and varmint shooters clean their rifle bores after every 10th or 20th shot. The bore should always be cleaned immediately after each shooting session, and left with a coat of preservative. This is less important where rimfire rifles are concerned, as most .22 rimfire bullets are pre-lubricated and leave no corrosive deposits. But even rimfire rifle barrels benefit from periodic, careful cleaning.

Choosing the right equipment is important. Even expert marksmen can't hit what they're shooting at when they use inaccurate rifles or defective sights. Poor accuracy isn't always the shooter's fault. Sometimes the equipment is to blame.

CHAPTER 4

.22 Rimfire: The Rifle You'll Never Outgrow

While some sportsmen feel they don't need anything other than a centerfire hunting rifle, the shooter serious about honing his or her skills will buy a .22 rimfire. A .22 is a must regardless of whatever centerfire rifles may be owned.

Many shooters get so much sheer, simple enjoyment from the .22 rimfires they started with that they never bother to buy a more costly centerfire. Several different types of target competition events are limited to rimfire rifles, including a 100-meter version of metallic silhouettes that's fun for the whole family.

For casual plinking, nothing beats the .22. Ammunition is so inexpensive that you can fire hundreds of rounds in an afternoon without denting the most frugal budget. In addition, rimfire rifles are extremely soft spoken, and generate absolutely no discernible recoil. They can be fired in abandoned gravel pits at the edge of town without creating a noise nuisance, although it's wise to check local ordinances first. You don't even need ear protectors to fire them comfortably.

Best of all, many rimfire rifles are capable of fine accuracy. The better-grade target models and many quality sporters will keep all their shots in the same hole at 75 feet or more. If you miss your target with a good .22, it usually isn't the rifle's fault.

Hunters of squirrels, rabbits and other small game find the .22 rimfire ideal

Rimfire rifles provide a lot of fun and low-cost plinking practice year-round. Most good shooters got their start with the little .22's and find them a relaxing way to get in some practice even after they have graudated to big-bore firearms.

for their purposes. Hollowpoint .22's are deadly on rodents and hares, while accurately placed head shots spoil no edible meat. The little .22 is diminutive, but deadly in the right hands.

While both centerfire and rimfire rifles have their fans, a well-rounded rifleman needs *both* rimfire and centerfire firearms. The two types complement each other. The sportsmen who consider .22 rifles firearms for youths and beginners are wrong. The .22 rimfire is a rifle you'll never outgrow.

How do you select the right rimfire? Frankly, there are so many good choices available the task isn't easy. But there are guidelines you can use to narrow the selection.

Again, the type of .22 you choose depends largely on your reasons for buying one. If you're primarily interested in target competition, there are a

You don't have to sacrifice quality just because you're buying a rimfire. This Kimber bolt-action is an excellent choice and a USA-made sporting arm.

number of rimfires admirably suited to the task. The West-German-made Anschutz rifle is available in several different target models. Remington, Mossberg, Harrington & Richardson, and Kimber all offer domestic target rifles, while other imports are marketed by Beeman and Interarms. Prices vary considerably, depending on model. It's possible to shoot tight groups with the budget-priced Mossberg, but top competitors are more likely to shoot more costly European rimfires.

Prices of rimfire bolt-actions can vary considerably. The full-stocked Anschutz at left is much higher priced than the domestic Savage-Stevens .22 shown at right.

Some target .22's such as this Anschutz Model 1813 are both costly and highly specialized. Top rimfire competitors are likely to use a European match rifle such as this.

There are special target models designed specifically for rimfire metallic silhouette competition, and these should be used with a good target scope of 8X or 10X magnification. The other target .22's will be paired with micrometer-adjustable aperture sights. Riflescopes are not allowed in most types of rimfire competition.

If formal target work isn't anticipated, you can select an action type to match your centerfire hunting rifles. If you own bolt-action deer and varmint rifles, select a bolt-action .22 for plinking and practice. Very fine bolt-action rimfire sporters are available from a number of manufacturers including Anschutz, Kimber, Sako, Ruger, and others. Good-quality bolt .22's can also be had from Harrington & Richardson, Marlin, Savage, and Mossberg.

Excellent .22 rimfire lever rifles are available from U.S. Repeating Arms (Winchester), Browning, and Marlin. These are all well-designed, high-quality firearms capable of very good accuracy.

Autoloaders are a favorite among small game hunters and plinkers. Weatherby, Ruger, Marlin, Mossberg, Browning, Remington, Charter Arms, Heckler & Koch, Savage, Anschutz, and Iver Johnson all offer selfloading .22's. Some auto rifles sport rougher, less refined triggers than you'll find on a good bolt-action .22 sporter, making tack-driving precision a little more difficult. But for most plinking and small game hunting purposes, a good autoloader offers adequate accuracy.

Slide-action .22's are available from Remington and Interarms. At one time the pump .22 was an American favorite, and most gun companies offered one or more models in this configuration. The two that still survive are very well-made little rifles. Fans of slide-action shotguns and Remington pump deer rifles are likely candidates for .22 pump ownership. These handy rifles are fast firing, and can be surprisingly accurate. Like the autoloader, they won't shoot with a top-quality bolt rifle, but they're more than adequate for most plinking activities.

There are a number of single-shot .22's on the market, including a few

The Marlin lever-action carbine is a highly popular rimfire used both for hunting and plinking.

top-quality target models. Excepting these target rifles, most one-shooters are intended for youthful beginners and are generally unsatisfactory for adult shooters. They're capable of good accuracy, but their one-shot capacity is too limiting for most experienced riflemen.

Once you've purchased a .22, it's a good idea to mount the same general type of sight that you'll be using on your centerfire rifles. If you favor an

Autoloading .22's such as this scoped Weatherby are favorites of both plinkers and small game hunters. This one has a tubular magazine that allows a lot of shooting without reloading.

open-sighted .30-30 lever carbine for use in the deer woods, by all means select an open-sighted rimfire of the same action type. Most riflemen today favor magnifying scope sights on rimfire and centerfire firearms alike.

By selecting a .22 rifle and sight that matches your centerfire rifle-sight combinations as closely as possible, you'll find that the handling skills gained with your rimfire are easily transferable to your larger centerfires. By practicing with one, you'll gain proficiency with the other. This is one reason every rifleman needs both a rimfire and centerfire model. Top marksmanship comes only through practice, and very few sportsmen could afford to shoot

It's a good idea to buy a rimfire rifle similar to the centerfire hunting rifles you use in the field. If you favor an open-sighted .30-.30 lever carbine in the deer woods, select a rimfire of the same action type. Being familiar with the mechanism of a gun promotes ease of handling and confidence.

enough factory centerfire ammunition to become truly proficient with their bigbore hunting rifles alone. Even reloaders would find the volume of ammo needed prohibitive in terms of cost.

Conversely, anyone can afford to shoot a rimfire rifle to his heart's content. Without low-cost .22 ammunition, very few shooters would gain expert status.

The .22 rimfire ammunition available today is of remarkable quality and consistency. There are three basic types of .22 long rifle loads to consider: standard-velocity target loads, high-velocity express loads, and the new hyper-velocity hunting loads. Very often the standard-velocity ammunition gives better accuracy than the high- and hyper-velocity fodder, but not always. Rimfire rifles can be almost as fussy regarding the loads they digest as centerfire rifles can. To be assured of the best possible accuracy, be sure to try several different brands and velocity levels.

There are three basic types of .22 Long Rifle loads available: standard-velocity target ammo, high-velocity hunting loads, and hyper-velocity rimfires. All can be fired from the same .22 rifle or handgun.

CHAPTER 5

How to Sight Your Rifle In

Before anyone can shoot well, he or she must first make sure the rifle is shooting where the sights are aimed. Getting your rifle properly sighted in is a necessity beginning shooters sometimes overlook; but it's something every expert does.

This is a job you should feel comfortable doing yourself—don't depend on a gunsmith or sporting goods store "mechanic" to handle the chore for you. Sighting a rifle in is really very easy. When it's done right, it doesn't require you to burn up a lot of costly ammunition, and it doesn't take a lot of time. When you're finished, you'll have the confidence of knowing your bullets will go exactly where you align your sights.

The basic sighting-in process is the same for both rimfire and centerfire rifles, although you'll adjust rimfire sights for a shorter distance. The same principles also apply whether you're using open iron sights, receiver-mounted aperture sights, or a magnifying scope. It's easier to adjust a scope to bring your rifle on target, as elevation and windage increments are clearly marked on the twin vertical and horizontal adjusting screws in the center turret. There's usually an arrow to indicate the direction the screw should be turned to move the bullet strike up or to the right. Each click or increment usually moves the strike ¼ or ½ inch at 100 yards.

Getting a rifle properly sighted-in is a prerequisite to any accurate shooting at game or targets. Adding a few clicks of elevation should bring this rifle right on target.

Receiver-mounted aperture sights are also micro-adjustable, with direction arrows found on many models. But sighting in a rifle equipped with standard factory-mounted open iron sights is a little more challenging. These sights typically feature rough step-adjustable elevation changes, and corrections in windage must often be made by tapping the rear sight sideways in its dovetail. A few open sights lack any convenient way to move the rear sight sideways, and the front sight must be moved instead. Obviously, these arrangements are crude compared to micrometer adjustments available in receiver or scope sights. Because you're forced to adopt a trial-and-error approach, zeroing an open-sighted rifle requires a bit more patience and time.

Once a rifle is zeroed in, you should re-check that zero periodically. A walnut stock can gain or lose moisture as humidity changes take place. This can make the point of impact change. Whenever you switch to a new brand of ammunition or to a different bullet weight, you should re-sight the rifle. If you're traveling by car, train or airplane to a distant hunting area, always fire a few rounds at a target to re-check the zero immediately after you arrive. Rifles and scopes can get bumped around considerably during travel, and this can

Williams open sights (left) and receiver-mounted aperture sight (right) are adjustable for both windage and elevation.

change the sight setting. Even if your rifle has remained untouched in the gun rack since last hunting season, you should take it to the shooting range and double check the sight setting before hunting with it again.

Fortunately, sighting in is a simple, straightforward process. You'll need some equipment: a few commercially printed or homemade targets (to make them yourself, simply draw a dark circle 2 to 4 inches in diameter on an 8½ x 11-inch sheet of white paper, then fill the circle in to create an easily visible aiming point), a screwdriver sized to fit the adjusting screws of your sight, a cardboard box to hold the targets, tape, or thumbtacks, and a supply of ammunition. Be sure the ammunition is of the proper caliber and is the same ammunition you'll be using for the shooting activity you have planned. Different brands and bullet weights seldom shoot to the same point of aim, and it's a waste of time and effort to sight a rifle in with a particular type of ammunition, then switch to another type for hunting or target shooting. This is a common mistake among economy-minded hunters who buy cheap military-surplus ammunition for the sighting-in session, then load up with an entirely different kind of load on the season opener.

You'll also need sandbags or some other kind of solid, but reasonably soft rest to help support your rifle while you shoot. If you don't have access to commercial sandbags you can make your own by simply filling a cloth sack or even a pair of old socks with dry, rock-free sand. A rolled-up sleeping bag or several blankets can also be used, although sandbags work best.

If you're sighting in a centerfire rifle, be sure to bring a set of ear protectors along. Without good ear protectors you're more likely to start flinching, and that introduces a significant source of possible error. Rimfire rifles are soft-spoken enough that hearing protectors aren't needed.

The actual sighting in should be done on a shooting range where you can place the target at least 100 yards away. Rimfire requirements are less de-

Rifles should be sighted-in from a comfortable benchrest position with the rifle supported by sandbags. Ear protectors should always be worn to help eliminate flinching and possible hearing damage.

manding, and a 50-yard range will suffice. If the range has a bench-type shooting rest, use it. Otherwise you should shoot from the prone position (described in chapter 2) with the rifle resting on sandbags or some other soft-sided rest. If you're using sandbags, you'll probably need to place a small box or some other object under the front sandbag to attain a comfortable height. Adjustable sandbag rests are available for bench-top use, but you can always improvise.

If you're sighting in a rifle with a newly attached scope sight, the first step is to make sure the scope is bore sighted. This should have been taken care of by the gunsmith who mounted the scope, but it's easy enough to check. If you mounted the scope yourself, boresighting is always necessary.

To bore-sight a bolt-action rifle, first remove the bolt so you can peer through the bore from the receiver end. To bore-sight a lever, pump, or autoloading rifle, you need a mirror device available from gunsmith suppliers.

Once the bolt has been removed, place the rifle in some kind of rest that will hold the firearm firmly horizontal. Next, find a knot on a fence, a light switch on the wall, or some other small object you can see through the bore. Position the rifle so that the object stays centered in the bore and anchor the rifle firmly in place. Then unscrew the protective caps covering the adjusting screws in the scope's central turret and look through the scope's eyepiece. Then turn the windage and elevation screws with a coin or screwdriver until the crosshairs move to center the same object you can see by looking through the bore. Your riflescope is now boresighted. Gunsmiths use an optical collimator to simplify this job, but there's no need to purchase one unless you intend to boresight several rifles and can afford the convenience of a collimator.

Boresighting is simply the first step in sighting your rifle in. All boresighting really accomplishes is to make sure your bullets will strike somewhere on target, not at 100 yards, but at the 25-yard mark.

Once you're at the range and have your rifle resting on some kind of firm support, place your first target 25 yards downrange from the muzzle. Then return, don your ear protectors, load a single round into the rifle's chamber, and adjust your sandbags (or other rest) until the crosshairs can be held steadily on target. Make sure you're comfortable before you shoot.

Take a deep breath, let it halfway out—then s-q-u-e-e-z-e the trigger, all the while making sure those crosshairs remain centered on the target. You should be taken by surprise when the rifle fires.

Hopefully, the bullet will make a hole somewhere on the target. If not, move the target 10 or 12 yards closer and try again. Then measure the horizontal and vertical distances from the bullet hole to the target's center.

Let's say the bullet strikes 4 inches to the right and 6 inches below the

Before sighting a rifle in with a new scope, make sure the scope is correctly bore-sighted. Here the author is using an optical collimator to do the job. There are ways, however, to do it without such tools.

It's a good idea to begin your shooting with a target only 25 yards downrange. This will give you a rough zero as you begin the sighting-in process. Make the final adjustments at 100 yards.

bullseye. This means you must move the crosshairs up and to the left to make the bullet strike where you want it. If your scope has ¼-minute adjustment gradations, it takes 4 "clicks" or increments to move the bullet strike 1 inch at 100 yards. Because your first shots are at only 25 yards, you need to dial in 4 times the adjustment you'd need at the longer range.

In other words, you need to turn the windage screw 4x4x4 turns to the left, and move the elevation screw up 4x4x6 turns. That's 64 clicks of left windage adjustment, and 96 clicks of positive elevation. You move the crosshairs in the *same* direction you want the bullet strike to move on the target.

Fire another round, again making sure the rifle is firmly supported by sandbags or whatever rest you're using. If further adjustments are needed, make them. Once you have the bullet striking within an inch or so of the target's center, it's time to move the target out to the 100-yard mark.

Repeat the process. Remember that you only need 4 clicks of adjustment to move the bullet 1 inch on the target at 100 yards (2 clicks if your scope has ½-minute gradations). Once you've moved the bullet strike to the center of the bullseye, fire a 3-shot group at that sight setting. Take your time between

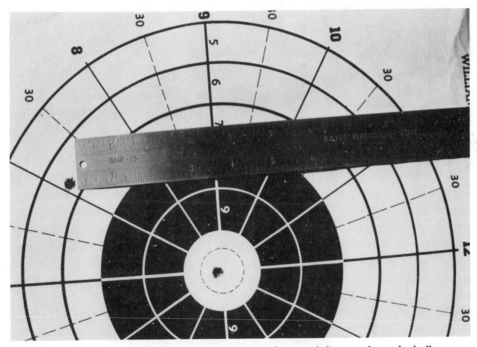

Once you've fired, measure the horizontal and vertical distance from the bullet hole to the center of the bull. Dial the right amount of windage and elevation adjustment and the next shot should be dead center.

Windage and elevation adjustment screws are located in the scope turret mid-way along the tube. Arrows point out the proper turning direction and adjustments are in stated increments for sighting-in at 100 yards.

shots, and make sure you have exactly the same sight picture each time. If your rifle is shooting accurately and you've done everything right, the result should be a tight, triangular-shaped group measuring less than 2 inches across.

For long-range hunting out to 250 yards or so, most sportsmen sight their centerfire rifles to print 2 or 2½ inches high at 100 yards. With modern, high-intensity cartridges like the .243 Winchester, .270, .30-06, and .300 magnums, that sight setting will allow you to hold "dead on" the heart-lung area of a deer-sized animal to 250 or 275 yards. Beyond that distance, you'll have to raise the crosshairs to compensate for bullet drop.

The same general principles apply for sighting in a rifle equipped with open iron or receiver sights. Move the rear sight in the *same* direction you want the bullet strike to move on target. If your rifle is shooting high and to the left, you need to move the rear sight down and right. If you must drift the rear sight sideways in its dovetail to make windage adjustments, use a drift punch made of soft brass, or even a block of wood. If you strike the barrel or sight with a steel tool, you'll mar the finish. Don't overdo things, either. It ordinarily takes only a soft tap or two to make a fair amount of windage adjustment. Take care not to knock the sight dovetail completely out of its slot.

If you must adjust the front sight, reverse the rule. The front sight should be moved or adjusted in the opposite direction you want the bullet strike to move.

When you install a receiver-mounted aperture sight as an aftermarket accessory, you may need to replace the front sight blade with one that's slightly taller or shorter. This can usually be determined at the time you purchase the receiver sight.

Because everyone sees his or her sights in a slightly different manner, only you can do a perfect job of sighting your own rifle in. No two people hold a rifle exactly alike. Some unconsciously cant the rifle to one side; others position their heads differently on the stock. These small, individual variations make a difference in where the bullet strikes on target.

Similarly, a riflescope that appears to be in focus for one shooter's eyes may provide a blurred sight picture for another's. To focus most riflescopes, simply unscrew the knurled ring immediately ahead of the eyepiece far enough to loosen it, then turn the eyepiece clockwise or counterclockwise while you look at some distant object. When the object appears in its sharpest focus, retighten the knurled ring. Be sure you don't back the eyepiece too far out, or it may detach from the scope tube and break the internal seals.

Getting your rifle properly sighted in is a prerequisite to any serious marksmanship. Unless you're sure the rifle is shooting where you aim, you can't be sure of hitting your target.

CHAPTER 6

Long-Range Marksmanship

The ability to hit a small target consistently at ranges of 300 to 400 yards or more is one thing that sets the expert rifleman apart from the average shooter. Such proficiency takes practice, but if you go about it in the right way you'll be able to shoot with the best of them at barrel-stretching distances.

Among hunters, the best long-range marksmen come from the varmint-shooting ranks. These sportsmen use heavy-barreled rifles chambered for fast-stepping .22, 6mm, or .25-caliber centerfires. These rifles are equipped with high-quality scopes of 10X, 12X, or greater magnification, and are likely used with a bipod or some other type of rest. Ammunition is often handloaded for greater accuracy, and each rifle is precisely sighted in.

With this kind of an outfit, an accomplished varmint hunter can hit the mark at surprising distances. He does this in spite of such annoyances as visual distortion caused by heat mirage, gusting winds, and hard-to-estimate yardage. In addition, the targets are under no obligation to remain stationary; they can drop to their feet and scamper off in any direction without warning.

Similarly, experienced sheep and mountain goat hunters regularly take trophies at 300 yards or beyond. Desert deer are sometimes shot at that distance, and such long shots are the rule with antelope.

One reason varmint and big-game trophy hunters are so successful at extended ranges is that they know how to take advantage of the terrain, and

When using a tree, rock,or other hard object as a rest to steady your rifle, make sure
your hand is between the hard object and your firearm to control bounce.

make the best use of boulders, trees, logs, or other improvised shooting
supports. Varmint shooters often use commercial bipods, sandbags or other
rests to help steady their rifles. These marksmen realize it makes sense to
eliminate as much human error as possible when shooting at distant game. It's
not cheating to use a rest. If you're not willing to take advantage of the firmest
support you can find, you should pass up those long hunting shots and try to
stalk closer. The most expert rifleman needs a rest to shoot ground squirrels or
prairie dogs at 350 or 400 yards.

There's a right way and a wrong way to use an improvised rest. Any stump,
log, tree limb, or boulder can be pressed into service, but be sure you don't rest
the riflestock or barrel directly against such unyielding supports. If rested
against any hard surface, the rifle will tend to jar away from that surface as it
fires. The vibrations created by the rapidly burning powder and the bullet as it
travels down the bore will make the rifle bounce at the hard contact point. As a
result, the bullet will fly off course.

Heavy-barreled varmint rifles equipped with high-magnification scopes and bi-pods make long-range shooting easier, more accurate, and therefore more enjoyable.

Always place your cradled hand, hunting cap, or jacket between the rifle and solid rest. The firearm must be cushioned from the hard surface before it's fired.

While a rest can be helpful from any shooting position—standing, kneeling, sitting, or prone—long-range shots should be attempted only from a low-profile stance. Prone is always the position preferred by extended distance marksmen. If there's no large rock or other natural rest handy, roll up a jacket or use a knapsack or pack to steady your rifle. Many shooters use a Harris bipod, a fold-down rest that quickly attaches to the sling swivel on your rifle's forend. When not in use, this bipod folds up against the barrel, where it's out of the way. The Harris bipod is available in two basic models—one with relatively long legs for shooting from the sitting position, and another adjustable for several prone heights.

Don't attempt any long shots while you're breathing hard or while your

Any stump, tree trunk or boulder can be used as a rifle rest, but remember that the gun should not be in direct contact with an unyielding object. Use something as a buffer.

Long shots should be attempted only from a low-profile position when hunting large game. Here the author uses a knapsack as an improvised rifle rest.

heart is pumping heavily. If you've been running or climbing, wait until you can control your pulse rate and get the scope's crosshairs to settle down before trying to shoot. If possible, take several deep, slow breaths and do your best to relax. Find a shooting position that's comfortable, then improvise some kind of firm rifle rest. Once you can keep the crosshairs steady on target, take a breath, let it halfway out and *s-q-u-e-e-z-e* the trigger.

One major problem in long-range shooting is determining how far the bullet will drop at extended distances. Gravity begins acting on a rifle bullet from the moment it exits the bore, pulling the bullet inexorably downward. To help compensate for this, riflescopes are mounted at a minute angle to the boreline. As a result, the bullet is aimed slightly upwards as it leaves the muzzle. It crosses the line of sight as viewed through the scope's reticle twice—once several yards from the muzzle as the bullet travels an upward path, and again somewhere between 100 and 200 yards downrange as the projectile falls toward earth. This path the bullet takes is called the bullet's trajectory.

If you examine the ballistics tables, you'll find some cartridges display much flatter trajectories than others. In other words, their bullets drop far less at extended ranges. As an extreme example, the factory 240-grain .44 Magnum load fired from a rifle zeroed to print dead on at 100 yards drops 65 inches at the 300-yard mark. With the same 100-yard zero, the 165-grain .30-06 factory load drops just 14.3 inches out at 300 yards. Obviously there's far less guess-work involved in hitting a target at 300 yards with the .30-06.

Since the bullet's path exactly coincides with the juncture of the crosshairs only twice, the rifle is precisely sighted in for only those two distances. At all other ranges the bullet will strike above or below the point of aim.

To hit game or some other target at extended range, you must do one of two things: first, you can sight your rifle to strike dead on at 100 yards, memorize the drop tables out to 300 or 400 yards, and then figure out how to accurately estimate the yardage to the target. It's easy if you're shooting on an established rifle range where target distances are obvious. Simply elevate the crosshairs the necessary height over the target and squeeze the trigger.

The other possibility is to use a rifle chambered for a very flat-shooting cartridge and sight it in so the bullet will strike point of aim at 200 or even 250 yards. If you've chosen the right cartridge and bullet weight, the bullet should rise only an inch or two above the sighting line out to zero range, and drop only a few inches at 300 yards or so. This means you can hold the crosshairs directly on the target and ignore the range factor as long as it doesn't exceed 300 yards.

For instance, the .22-250 Remington is a very popular round among varmint shooters, primarily because it has a very flat trajectory. Federal's 40-grain hollowpoint factory load in this caliber can be sighted to print at point of aim at 250 yards. This places the bullet just 2 inches high at 100 yards, 1.8 inches high at 200 yards, dead on at 250, and only 3.2 inches below at 300 yards. This makes it theoretically possible to center the crosshairs on a standing prairie dog and hit it at any range out to 300 yards without raising or lowering the rifle or changing the sight picture in any way. This eliminates the need to figure the range until the animal is more than 300 yards away.

At 400 yards that same .22-250 load would drop 15.5 inches, while out at 500 yards the drop is nearly 40 inches. Between 400 and 500 yards, guessing wrong on range distance by only 50 yards would result in a clean miss.

Deer-sized animals present a much larger target. If you sight almost any modern rifle in the .270 Winchester—.30-06 class to print between 2 and 2½ inches high at 100 yards, you should be able to drop game cleanly out to 275 yards or so with no sight holdover. Beyond that distance, it's usually advise-able to pass up the shot and get closer.

This rifle has a Harris bipod with legs that adjust to accommodate a sitting shooter. His partner watches for dust strikes to indicate bullet placement on a prairie-dog hunt.

Portable rangefinders are available for hunting, but it's often tough to get precise readings at long ranges.

There are portable rangefinding devices designed for hunters. These use the binocular principle to superimpose two images in the viewer's eyepiece as he turns a knob. Once the images coincide, the user simply reads the range from a dial. In theory such rangefinders are a fine idea, but I've found these devices less than practical in the field. It's difficult to get exact, repeatable readings from the small, portable rangefinders now available. I once took a careful reading on a distant rock formation, then asked two companions to do the same. The readings varied from 240 to 450 yards. I've also taken consecutive readings from an object several hundred yards away, and had the results vary by more than 160 yards. The rangefinder is just one more thing to carry afield, and many animals aren't patient enough to stand around posing while you fiddle with it.

There are also several rangefinding scopes on the market, and these are a bit more practical. Most of these scopes are variable-power models with a set of parallel stadia hairs visible in the reticle. The stadia hairs move closer together or farther apart as you change magnification. By knowing the body depth of the animal you're hunting, you can make a pretty good stab at estimating the range to that animal if you can find one willing to pose for you. Some systems are predicated on the theory that the deer-sized target will measure approximately 18 inches from back to breastbone. When the stadia hairs bracket the chest from top to bottom, you can read the distance to the animal. Other rangefinding reticles use a center dot of known size for this kind of comparison.

Several rangefinding scopes take things a step further by automatically raising the crosshair to compensate for bullet drop. You simply bracket the animal with the stadia hairs, place the aiming crosshairs midway up the chest cavity and squeeze the trigger.

Again, these devices operate on the theory that all the animals you shoot at will have standardized body depth dimensions, and that you'll have time to tinker with the scope before your trophy trots off. These scopes also lead riflemen to assume an optical and mechanical precision that in fact may not be present.

While rangefinding/trajectory compensating scopes are far from perfect, they do offer an alternative to blind guessing when it comes to estimating yardage. In that respect, they're of certain value, but I'm not a fan of rangefinding and trajectory compensating scopes because they often tempt hunters into shooting at extreme distances far beyond their marksmanship abilities.

Consistently precise sighting is important in all kinds of rifle shooting, and it's particularly critical at long range. If the point of impact wanders, check your scope-mounting screws to make sure they're tight.

Trying for small rodents at an extended range causes no harm, as the animal is either missed completely or killed cleanly. The same doesn't apply for big game, however, and sportsmen should use caution in attempting any shot that could increase the chance of crippling the animal.

No harm comes in trying 500 or even 600-yard shots at ground squirrels or prairie dogs. With targets that tiny, the results are either sudden death or a clean miss. But when you're shooting at an elk, deer, or even an antelope at those ranges, the odds are heavy you'll only wound the animal.

I believe 300 yards is a long shot when you're hunting deer-sized game. Anytime you exceed that distance, the chances of a clean kill drop dramatically. Even if you're confident of your marksmanship, you should try to stalk closer. Such are the demands of sportsmanship.

As I've noted earlier in this chapter, it's possible to sight most modern rifles in to allow you to hold dead on target out to nearly 300 yards. So if you limit your shots to ranges of 275 yards or less, you don't really need a long-distance rangefinder.

How do you determine whether your target is closer or farther away than 275 yards? The best way I know is to visualize a football field, which measures an even 100 yards between end zones. See how many football fields you can imagine lying end-to-end between you and the target. It's also helpful to do a

With a modern, flat-shooting rifle sighted-in to print 2½ inches or so high at 100 yards, no holdover is required on deer-sized game out to 250 or 275 yards.

lot of target practice at known ranges of 100 and 200 yards. If you do this, it's not too difficult to judge whether that trophy buck is within reasonable range (250-275 yards) or too far away.

A stunt I periodically try afield is to try to estimate the yardage to some distant object I'm walking toward. Then I count my long paces to check my guess. This kind of practice is invaluable when it comes to estimating range.

A common mistake some hunters make in steep, mountain country is to figure the line-of-sight distance to the target, and adjust the sight picture accordingly. This can cause the shot to go high, particularly at extended range. If you're shooting up (or down) at a steep angle, you're apt to aim too high to allow for bullet drop. Remember, the bullet drops only in accordance with the *horizontal* distance between yourself and the target.

That's yet another argument against attempting hunting shots at extreme ranges. If your rifle is sighted to print 2 or 2½ inches high at 100 yards (with a flat-shooting cartridge), you needn't worry about how gravity will affect trajectory if you know your game is within 275 years measured along your line of sight. Then you can forget about shooting angles and trigonometry.

Both wind and mirage can play a part in long-range shooting. A strong side wind can cause a bullet to move several inches off target as it travels down-range. The cure for this is to move the crosshairs upwind of the target. Only experience can tell you how far to hold off the mark—this depends on how far away the target is; the size, shape, and speed of your bullet; and the angle and velocity of the wind.

Generally speaking, only long-distance varmint shooters will need to concern themselves with the wind factor. They're shooting at a tiny mark, and a bullet blown several inches off course will be a clean miss. Deer or elk present a much larger vital-area target, and are usually shot at ranges short of 300 yards. This makes pinpoint precision less mandatory. Competitive target shooters also need to learn to cope wind and this comes with practice.

To cope with high, gusting winds, varmint hunters should have a partner watch the target with binoculars or a spotting scope. When a shot is fired, the coach should carefully watch for the puff of dust caused by the bullet strike. He can then advise how far right or left of the target the shooter should move his sights.

Mirage can be a problem. Moisture evaporating from the ground or heat waves shimmering from the plain or a hot rifle barrel interfere with a sharp sight picture. The longer the distance, the greater mirage will affect your shooting. Mirage itself is caused by the air close to the ground being more

Always pad a hard rest with something soft. This shooter is using both a hat and a sandbag to ensure a steady shot from a fencepost rest.

dense than the air above. It's more noticeable on hot, clear days, and there's not a lot you can do about it. In the summertime, you're likely to have to deal with either wind or mirage, but seldom both at the same time.

If there's a secret to long-range marksmanship, it's finding a firm rest and assuming a low, solid, shooting position behind it. Then take your time, use proper breath control, and carefully squeeze off your shot. If your rifle has been properly sighted in and you've judged the range correctly, you should hit what you're shooting at.

The only kind of shooting where long-range marksmanship is attempted regularly from the unstable offhand position is centerfire rifle metallic silhouette target competition. In this game, only the standing position is allowed. Life-sized metallic silhouettes of chickens, javelina, turkey, and sheep are shot at ranges between 200 and 500 meters.

Hitting a sheep-sized target at 500 meters from the offhand stance takes practice. Most experienced silhouette riflemen assume a slightly modified standing position, with the left hip thrust forward and the left (supporting) elbow and upper arm pressed against the body for added support. Surprising scores have been fired from this position.

With the exception of this type of target work, long-range riflemanship should always be aided by some kind of supporting rest.

CHAPTER 7

How to Hit Running Game

Some people feel a rifle should be used only on stationary targets, particularly in the field. Admittedly, your chance of connecting is much better when the target holds obligingly still. But once an animal is aware of your presence he's going to move. As a result, the only shot often offered is at running game.

Because running shots at some game are so common, certain countries won't issue a hunting license until the applicant proves he can hit a moving target. I hunted moose in Finland a few years back, and had to hit a bullseye on a lifesize moose silhouette as it traveled sideways along a track at a realistically fast clip. The target had to be hit 3 consecutive times as the cardboard moose ran back and forth along its track. The shooting was done offhand from 100 meters, and if you missed the bullseye once you didn't get your license.

At that distance and speed, I found you had to hold a sustained lead of about two feet to land your shots in the bullseye. By "sustained lead," I mean you had to keep the crosshairs two feet in front of the bullseye while you kept your rifle moving with the target. The other technique commonly used to hit a moving target with a rifle is the "point and shoot" method. With this method, you aim your sights at some point ahead of the running animal, hold the rifle steady, and shoot. If you've picked the right aiming point and timed your shot correctly, your bullet and the animal should meet.

In Finland and some other countries, an applicant for a hunting license must prove his shooting ability. This fast-moving moose target is set up to test a hunter's ability to hit running game.

Because your rifle is being pointed at a stationary spot and the animal is running toward it, "point and shoot" marksmanship requires a greater lead. It takes time for you to make the decision to shoot, for that message to be carried from your brain to your trigger finger, for the finger to squeeze (not jerk) the trigger, and for the spring mechanism to drive the firing pin forward to dent the primer and ignite the propellent powder inside the cartridge case. It takes a few milliseconds of additional time for the bullet to exit the rifle and travel downrange to the planned meeting point. All the while a deer, antelope, or jackrabbit is covering ground at his best escape velocity.

When you use the "sustained lead" method, you need only concern yourself with how far the animal will travel after the bullet is on its way. By keeping the rifle moving to match the animal's speed, you needn't try to consider your own reaction time or the rifle's lock time (the time it takes for the mechanical parts to complete their task). This allows a much smaller lead.

How much lead is actually required with either method? It's impossible to say, because everyone has different reaction times, and each rifleman sees the target differently. As a rule, most running targets are missed because *not*

This Finnish rifleman takes his shots at the running moose target, at 100 meters. If you don't qualify, you don't get to hunt.

enough lead is allowed. Even experienced deer and antelope hunters regularly fail to hold the sights far enough ahead of a running trophy. They simply find it difficult to believe that the animals can move so fast. This is particularly true of antelope, even though most hunters know that pronghorns have been clocked at speeds approaching 60 miles per hour. That's 88 feet per second. When hunters shoot at fleeing antelope, misses generally show as puffs of dust several lengths behind the target animal.

Another factor complicating estimated lead is the angle the target is moving in relation to your position. An animal quartering toward you or away will obviously require a smaller lead than one running broadside, or at right angles to the shooter. An animal running directly away requires no lead at all unless he's running up or downhill, in which case you must raise or lower your sights to compensate.

Many running shots are offered at very close range, and this can cause problems for the rifleman with a high-magnification scope. Scopes of 4X, 6X, or 8X magnification offer relatively small viewing fields—and the greater the magnification, the smaller the field of view. For instance a 6X scope may have a field of view that covers 23 feet at 100 yards. On the other hand, a variable-

This drawing shows an example of lead on a running deer. You must aim ahead of the animal in such situations, and the amount of lead necessary depends on the angle and speed at which the animal is traveling.

power 1¾X-5X scope of the same make may offer a field of view measuring 66 feet across at the 100-yard mark when its magnification is at its lowest setting.

Obviously, a shooter will have an easier time finding a close, moving target with the wider field of view. With low-power variable models set at 1½X magnification, it's possible for a rifleman to view the target with both eyes fully open. This gives you the full binocular effect even when one eye is looking through the scope reticle. That lets you find and get on the target extremely fast, and it's one reason hunters of dangerous game often favor low-powered scopes. If an animal charges at close range, you need to be able to place the crosshairs on target immediately.

Because target movement introduces yet another factor that contributes to missing, you should try to keep the other factors at a minimum. For anything but point-blank shots, assume a solid sitting or even prone position rather than shoot standing up. As the range increases, the likelihood of missing also rises, even when the target stands perfectly still. This means you should avoid

Deer spooked in this kind of cover will likely provide a close, running target. These situations separate the neophyte or poor shot from those who knew how to shoot fast and instinctively.

taking any long-range running shots. The risk of wounding and losing an animal is too great when the animal presents a running, bouncing target at 300 yards or so.

On the other hand, a deer bolting at 40 or 50 yards is relatively easy to hit. You don't need a lot of lead at that range, and you don't have time to plot the deer's path or rate of speed. When you shoot reflexively, you're more likely to hit what you're aiming at, at least at close range.

You can't learn how to hit a running animal by simply reading a book. You must shoot and practice on moving targets. Have someone roll an old tennis ball in front of you while you shoot at it with a .22 rimfire. Improvise your own

For anything other than point-blank range, assume a solid sitting or prone position before shooting. You usually have more time than you think.

If you can hit a bouncing jackrabbit with a .22 rifle, running deer should be no problem. This hunter missed, as the dust puff shows.

moving targets and practice with them. A friend and I once rigged a cardboard bullseye inside an old tire, and took turns rolling it down a steep hillside. This provided excellent practice. The tire rolled and bounced unpredictably, and moved fast enough to simulate the speed of frightened game.

Another excellent exercise is to hunt running jackrabbits with either a centerfire deer rifle or a rimfire .22. If you can hit a bouncing jack at 50 or 60 yards, downing a running deer at that distance should pose no problem. Remember to lead each animal, and note whether a missed shot puffs up dust ahead of or behind the moving target. It may surprise you to learn just how far you need to lead what you're shooting at.

Learn to shoot with both eyes open. Many riflemen habitually close the weak eye when aiming. If you're using a high-magnification scope you'll have to get along with one eye—but with iron sights or a low-powered scope, binocular vision lets you find the target faster.

The only way you can learn to hit running game consistently is to practice on other moving targets. Some shooting clubs hold "running boar" shoots, and have moving targets available. Other rifle ranges offer "running deer" target facilities. If you belong to a club with an established rifle range, it's possible to

Learn to shoot with both eyes open, even when using a scope. Binocular vision lets you find the target faster.

build your own "running target" facilities with a little effort and imagination. One low-cost arrangement I saw a few years ago consisted of nothing more than a clothesline-like wire suspended at a steep angle across the range. Weighted targets were hung from pulleys, and were allowed to speed down the stretched line under the force of gravity.

You *can* learn to hit running game—but it takes practice.

CHAPTER 8

Everyone Wins in Target Competition

Every rifleman can benefit from participating in target competition. Whether you're engaged in a friendly plinking match or shooting in a more formal, NRA-sanctioned meet, you can learn a lot about your skills and shortcomings. Competition can make you a better shot.

If you don't feel you're ready for serious paper-punching competition, you can shoot in metallic silhouette matches. Centerfire matches are conducted throughout the country with riflemen shooting offhand at lifesized steel silhouettes of chickens, pigs, turkeys, and sheep. The targets are set at ranges from 200 to 500 meters, and the target must fall down when hit. Silhouettes that only spin, or are shot out of turn don't count.

You can use any hunting-type centerfire rifle of 6mm (.243-inch) or greater caliber. Maximum rifle weight is 10 pounds 2 ounces. Any kind of sights may be used, and most shooters favor riflescopes.

No accessories such as shooting gloves, padded rifle jacket, adjustable buttplate, palm rest, sling, or anything else that might serve as an artificial rest or otherwise aid the shooter may be used.

Centerfire silhouette matches are held both by local clubs and on a national or regional basis. Be sure to try a few local shoots before you enter any of the larger matches. The competition is keen, and the large events attract Olympic-class marksmen.

Metallic animal silhouettes that clang and fall over when hit provide more excitement than paper targets both for participants and spectators. These are the small silhouettes designed for .22 target fun.

An even better starting point is rimfire silhouette. These matches are shot using .22 rimfire rifles, with the farthest targets being set only 100 meters away. The silhouettes are 1/5 the scale of the larger centerfire targets. The smallest target is the chicken, which is placed 40 meters (or paces) from the firing line. The javelina, or pig-shaped silhouettes are set at 60 meters, while the turkey cutouts are 77 meters downrange. The ram silhouettes are shot at 100 meters.

Each target has its own steel base, and is painted flat white to help the silhouettes stand out against a dirt background. The white paint also shows hits clearly, which helps determine questionable calls.

In rimfire competition, each contestant fires at five targets at each of the four ranges. You repeat this for a complete course in which 40 shots are fired. Only one shot is allowed at each silhouette, and each must be fired at in its

You have to do more than just make the metal target clang; bullet placement is
important to make the target fall over. If it doesn't drop, you don't score.

proper turn, left to right. If you miss, be sure to move on to the next target in
line for the next shot.

Additional information can be obtained from the National Rifle Association, 1600 Rhode Island Ave., N.W., Washington, DC 20036. *The Silhouette
Handbook*, which has target patterns and other information, can be purchased at nominal cost by writing the NRA Sales Department. You can also
order a rules and regulation booklet. To obtain applications for regional or
national matches, write the NRA's Silhouette Department.

Because rimfire silhouette shooting requires a bare minimum of
equipment—all you need are some steel targets, a .22 rifle and a supply of

Note the size of the targets here. They're actually 1/5th the size of those used for centerfire competition. These ram silhouettes set at 100 meters are the most distant for .22 matches.

ammunition—you can hold your own matches with very little expense. You can make your own targets from sheet steel using patterns available from the NRA, or buy them from a number of suppliers who make them commercially. A set of rimfire targets will last a lifetime, and need no upkeep other than periodic spray painting. Shoots can be held anywhere you can find a 100-meter shooting range with a safe backstop.

One reason I recommend rimfire silhouette target shooting for those serious about attaining expert status is that firing at the animal-shaped targets that clang and fall over when hit is a lot more fun than shooting at paper bullseyes. This means you're more likely to practice regularly, and matches are more interesting for shooters and spectators alike.

Centerfire metallic silhouette is also fun and highly entertaining, but centerfire rifles and ammunition are considerably more expensive. You also need a 500-meter range for competitive matches, and such facilities are harder to find than the 100-meter spaces required for rimfire shoots. Another reason metallic

You can find matches sponsored by the National Rifle Association throughout the country. Contact the NRA for information on any that might be available in your area. Also check the sports-shop bulletin boards, and local outdoor columns in your newspaper for leads if you want to get in on competitive shooting.

silhouette competition is so helpful is that you're required to shoot from the relatively unsteady offhand position. If you can learn to hit targets while you're standing up, you shouldn't have any trouble displaying expert marksmanship from the kneeling, sitting, or prone positions.

Shooting at paper targets is also instructive and available at both indoor and outdoor ranges. Check the Yellow Pages under "Gun Clubs," or ask at your local sporting goods store or gun shop to learn where and how to get started in organized shooting matches. Writing the NRA can also be extremely helpful.

If less formal competition has more appeal, create your own plinking, metallic silhouette, or target shoots. Friendly competition with one or more companions is more fun than shooting solo, and you can critique each other on form and technique.

Competition adds incentive for you to practice—and the more you practice, the better marksman you become. As you work on muscle and breath control, bullseyes will come with increasing frequency. Don't begrudge any time spent at the target range. If you pay attention to what you're doing and concentrate on hitting increasingly smaller marks, you can't help but become a better shot.

Competing with other shooters gives you an invaluable means of comparison. You can gauge your progress by matching your scores against the marks of serious riflemen.

Don't be afraid to ask more experienced shooters for their advice. Most marksmen are happy to spend a few minutes coaching less experienced riflemen, and the tips you gain can be invaluable. Are you holding your rifle right? Is your supporting arm directly under the forend? Is your stance comfortable and well balanced? Do you flinch even slightly when your firing pin clicks unexpectedly against an empty chamber or fired cartridge case? These are things you can determine for yourself, but another rifleman may be able to spot such mistakes with greater ease. The place to find real experts is on the firing line at formal shooting matches. If you really want to become an expert, you should spend some time there yourself.

CHAPTER 9

How to Beat "Buck Fever"

Some sportsmen who are cool, calm, and collected at the practice range have trouble staying that way when they have game in their sights.

This can be attributed to a temporary malady known as "buck fever." The illness strikes without warning—usually as you're lining up your sights on a trophy deer with a rocking-chair rack, or any large animal you may be hunting. When the madness grips you, you may shiver uncontrollably, develop a pounding pulse and hammering heart rate, or simply feel a sudden need to sit down and rest.

The symptoms may be even more extreme. More than one hunter stricken with buck fever has levered all the cartridges from his rifle without firing a shot. I actually watched one companion do exactly that. Every time he levered a fresh cartridge into the chamber, he'd take hurried aim, utter a loud "bang," and eject the unfired round. After the deer had disappeared, the only way I could convince him he'd acted so strangely was to point at the live ammunition littering the ground at his feet.

Victims of buck fever may not be aware of the affliction, and appear to act normally. They take careful aim, slowly *s-q-u-e-e-z-e* the trigger—and miss. Usually fine marksmen may miss several times at what amounts to point-blank range, then shake their heads in wonder as the deer bounce away

The mere sight of a shootable deer can bring on a serious dose of "buck fever." It's something you can control, however, as this chapter explains.

A big rack suddenly jumping out of this cover could set a hunter to shaking. Buck fever can strike any time, and even experienced hunters are occasionally affected.

unhurt. Those seemingly bulletproof deer you hear of were most likely shielded by a low-grade case of buck fever.

Sufferers aren't limited to deer hunters only. Buck fever visits hunters of antelope, elk, moose, caribou, mountain sheep, bear, and other large game. It has even been known to attack pheasant hunters and other upland game enthusiasts. Not a few waterfowlers have been afflicted when faced with their first goose at close range.

To some degree, buck fever is an integral, even desirable part of hunting. The day you *don't* get excited when you see a trophy buck or watch a flight of honkers glide toward your decoys is probably the day you'll begin spending less time afield and more hours in front of the television set. Hunting is *supposed* to set your pulse racing every now and then.

The trick is to keep that excitement under at least partial control. You don't want to miss an easy shot because you couldn't hold the sights steady. Or worse yet, become so excited you mistake a cow, horse, or even another hunter for game. Sportsmen are wounded and killed every year by overeager idiots who later swear they were "shooting at deer."

Simply speaking, if buck fever has you in its grip, you don't want to shoot until you've calmed down and have your excitement under control. If you inexplicably can't hold the sights steady, lower the rifle from your shoulder, take a deep breath, exhale and do your best to relax. Let your muscles go limp for a few seconds. Remember, there are other deer (or elk, or antelope), and if you don't bag the one you're looking at you'll have other chances. Try to keep things in proper perspective.

One excellent way to avoid buck fever is to become a trophy hunter. This means you don't excitedly shoot the first legal buck that comes along. Instead, you take the time to examine its rack carefully through binoculars. Take a spotting scope along and evaluate potential trophies at a distance. Being more selective helps you remain calmer, and gives you time to keep your emotions under better control.

Never be in too great a hurry. Even if you jump a buck from its bed, there's usually plenty of time to bring the rifle up and get your sights on target. Buck fever often makes you too anxious to get a shot away, and a hurried shot is likely to miss.

Shotgunners have the same problem. I can't count the ducks, geese, and pheasants I've missed simply because I was too excited to take my time. I've seen a lot of seemingly pellet-proof birds in my years of hunting. Most were spared by a too-quick trigger finger.

When you first feel the grip of buck fever, slow down and do your best to

Buck fever isn't limited to deer hunters. The sight of your first big Canada goose gliding toward your decoys or soaring straight toward your pit can lead to a shot that hits nothing but air. It's frustrating, but you can reduce the possibilities for errant shots.

To combat buck fever, take your time and do your best to keep the excitement under control. It may sound easier than it is, but continued hunting experience in a variety of situations is a big help. Note that this hunter has taken the time to get himself into a steady position.

If buck fever does strike, lower your rifle from your shoulder, take a deep breath, and try to get control of yourself and the situation.

relax. Lower your sights for a second or two, and take that deep breath. Remember, you *can* afford a brief pause. Look for a handy rest to steady your aim. If you're shooting a shotgun, make sure your feet are solidly placed.

If that treatment fails and you miss anyway, remember that it's not the end of the world. There'll be another buck or bird, and you'll get another chance to conquer the fever!

CHAPTER 10

Handgunning Basics

Handguns are by far the most difficult firearms to master. Unlike rifles and shotguns, handguns are held at arm's length. There's no stock to help steady the gun against the shoulder and spread recoil.

Holding a 2- or 3-pound weight at the end of your outstretched arm becomes tiring in a hurry. At first it seems impossible to hold a firearm steady in that position. It seems equally unlikely you'll ever be able to hit what you shoot at.

Fortunately, almost anyone can learn to shoot a handgun well. It takes a little time and practice, but if you go about it in the right way you can soon become proficient in the use of pistol or revolver.

The first thing a handgunner should do is learn to concentrate on safety. The same safety rules listed in chapter 2 apply, and these should be reviewed before you ever pick up a handgun. Because pistols and revolvers have relatively short barrels, it's much easier to injure yourself accidentally with a handgun than it is with a rifle or shotgun. The importance of always keeping the muzzle pointed in a safe direction takes on even greater urgency when it comes to using handguns. Those short barrels have a very short turning radius; it takes continuous, concentrated effort to keep them pointing harmlessly away.

Years ago the acceptable stance for shooting a handgun was to stand facing away from the target at some 45 degrees, and extend the shooting hand as far as possible away from the body. Only one hand was used to hold the gun; the

78

The one-handed standing position is used in many formal kinds of handgun competition. It takes practiced muscle control to shoot offhand effectively.

other was allowed to hang loosely at the shooter's side, or placed in a handy pocket to keep it out of the way.

This is still the stance used in many formal kinds of handgun competition. Once you've mastered it, it's possible to score surprisingly well from this relatively unsteady position. But it takes stamina and practiced muscle control to shoot well one-handed.

We now live in a more enlightened age, and most handgunners happily grip their firearms in both hands. What's more, they shoot from a wide variety of kneeling, sitting, and prone positions. Field gunners also take cheerful advantage of any available rest.

As a result, pistol and revolver shooters are consistently hitting targets at longer ranges. It takes less time to develop decent marksmanship skills, and interest in the handgun has markedly increased. Hunters of both large and small game have adopted the handgun, and pistol-toting plinkers abound. Shooting metallic game silhouette targets with a handgun has become a highly popular, fast-growing sport.

There are three basic types of handguns: auto pistols, revolvers, and single shots. Auto pistols are flat, slab-sided guns fed from a removable magazine located within the grip, or butt. They feature a reciprocating breechblock, and most have a manually operated, mechanical safety.

Revolvers hold their ammunition supply in a revolving cylinder located immediately behind the barrel. Western-styled single-action sixguns must be manually cocked by pulling back the hammer before each shot. Their cylind-

Auto pistols are flat, slab-sided guns fed from a removeable magazine located in the grip.

ers are loaded one round at a time through a loading gate on the right side. Modern double-action revolvers can be fired by simply pulling the trigger, or by manually cocking them first. Large magnum revolvers are potent enough to hunt deer-sized and larger game. Revolvers have no manually operated external safeties.

Single-shot handguns hold but one round of ammunition at a time. These are typically long-barreled guns with strong turnbolt or break-top actions. Single-shot pistols are designed for long-range accuracy, and many are cham-

Revolvers contain their ammo in a revolving cylinder behind the barrel. Large magnums are potent enough to hunt deer-sized game.

bered for high-intensity rifle rounds. Single shots are popular with many hunting handgunners, as well as metallic silhouette target shooters.

Whichever type of handgun you choose, you should be sure you know how to safely load, unload, and operate it before taking it to the shooting range. Most new handguns are accompanied by written instructions. If these are lacking, have the salesman who sold you the gun show you how to operate it, or enlist the aid of an experienced handgunner.

With these basics behind you, it's time to learn how to hold a handgun properly and assume a steady, practical shooting stance.

The steadiest way to support a handgun is to firmly grasp the grip in the shooting hand, with the hand as high as possible on the grip. If you're shooting an auto pistol, the web between the thumb and forefinger should be forced upwards against the curved section of the backstrap. Positioning your hand high on the grip aids control by putting the support in line with the direction of recoil. It also makes for a more solid grip.

The fingers should be wrapped firmly around the butt. The index finger should contact the trigger near the center of the pad forward of the first joint—*not* at the joint itself. The joint is less sensitive than the fingertip, and provides less control. You may need to contact the trigger farther back on the finger when shooting double-action, as the long, double-action pull requires greater strength and pressure.

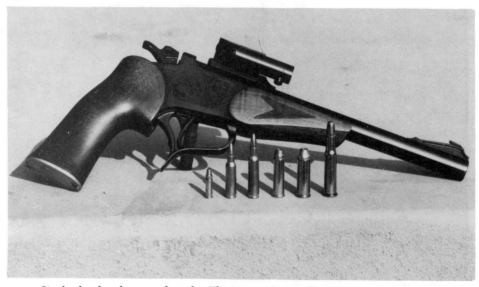

Single-shot handguns such as this Thompson/Center Contender are chambered for a variety of high-intensity hunting loads.

The two-handed overlapping grip is recommended for most handgun shooting.

Take a firm grip, but don't squeeze too hard. If you apply too much pressure (enough to whiten the knuckles) the gun will start to shake. Simply hold the gun firmly, with authority.

When you have the gun properly positioned in the shooting hand, wrap the other hand around the grip with the fingers overlapping the fingers of the shooting hand. The thumb should *not* wrap around the grip, but should point forward along with the other fingers of the supporting hand. If this thumb is wrapped high around the grip of an autoloader, it'll be in the path of the reciprocating slide.

Some gunners prefer to rest the gun and shooting hand in the palm of the support hand. The fingers of the supporting hand are then wrapped up and around the shooting hand. This offers a certain degree of support, but lacks the rigidity of the recommended wrap-around style where both wrists are more or less parallel.

To shoot offhand using the two-handed hold, face your target with your feet a comfortable distance apart. If you're shooting right-handed, your left foot should be slightly forward. Stand erect, and hold the gun at arm's length in front of you.

The right (shooting arm) elbow should be locked, while the elbow of the supporting arm may be locked or slightly bent. The supporting arm should

Some gunners prefer to rest the gun and shooting hand in the palm of the support hand. This offers some support, but isn't as rigid as the recommended wrap-around style.

then be moved rearward to provide stabilizing pressure to the shooting hand and arm.

Raise the gun to eye level, moving the shoulder of your shooting arm upwards. Lower your head until the side of your chin is in firm contact with that shoulder. Make sure the gun is straight up and down, and not canted to either side. Lean slightly forward into the gun to increase stability.

When you aim at the target, you'll find it impossible to keep the front sight, rear sight, and target in simultaneous focus. If you're shooting at a round bullseye, it's always best to let the target blur slightly and focus on the sights.

The standing, two-handed hold just described is known as a modified Weaver stance. This is a highly useful position for handgunners; it's very stable, as well as fast and easy to assume. Combat shooters use a similar position, but with their knees bent to provide a much lower profile.

Even greater stability is offered by the sitting, kneeling, and prone positions. In the kneeling stance, a right-handed shooter kneels on his right knee

To shoot offhand using the two-handed hold, stand facing the target. The elbow of the shooting arm should be locked as shown here.

and rests his left elbow just forward of the upraised left knee. The right arm is extended with the elbow locked, while the left, or supporting arm is bent at the elbow. The shooter sits on the heel of his right foot, which is perpendicular to the ground.

In the sitting position, the upper arms (not the elbows) rest in the hollows alongside each knee. If the arms or elbows are rested on top of the knees there will be less stable support.

To assume the sitting position, simply sit facing the target with both knees raised. Hold the gun in the two-handed grip described above, and lean forward. Rest the lower part of each upper arm immediately above the elbow (not the elbow itself) in the hollow alongside each knee. In this position, both elbows will be bent.

To shoot from prone, lie on your stomach and spread your legs a comfortable distance apart, insteps pressed toward the ground. The line made by your body should point toward the target. Again, hold the gun two-handed, and extend both arms toward the target. Both elbows should be bent to carry the gun's weight. Raise your head sufficiently to allow you to align the sights with the target. This is a very steady shooting position in spite of the fact that wrists and elbows aren't locked.

The same kind of breathing and trigger control used in rifle shooting (see chapter 2) are used in handgunning. Take a deep breath, exhale part way, and squeeze the trigger. If you're using a double-action revolver or auto pistol, it should be manually cocked (to put it in the single-action mode) before you

The prone position is extremely stable, and is recommended for long-range shooting in the field.

Double-action revolvers should be manually cocked before shooting if you're looking for top accuracy.

fire if you're after the best accuracy. Double-action auto pistols automatically reload and cock themselves after the first shot is fired. In other words, only the first round is fired double-action if you fail to manually cock the hammer. The remaining rounds in the magazine will be triggered single-action. If you're shooting a double-action revolver, the hammer should be manually cocked before each shot for optimum accuracy. Double-action trigger pulls are much heavier and harder to control.

Once you have the four basic shooting positions mastered, you should learn to adapt them to take advantage of natural supports like trees, stumps, and large boulders. Such supports aren't permissible in most kinds of handgun competition, but they can be invaluable when hunting.

No part of the handgun should be allowed to bear directly against any hard, unyielding rest. If you rest the barrel or frame against any hard object, the gun will jar away from the point of contact when it fires. Always cradle the gun in both hands, then steady your hands against any available support. If you're shooting a hard-recoiling magnum, it's advisable to wear gloves to prevent tree limbs, stumps, or other natural rests from abrading the skin.

Ear protection is doubly important when shooting handguns. The short barrel intensifies muzzle blast, and the increased noise can seriously affect accuracy and control. Shooting bigbore handguns without adequate ear protection will cause permanent hearing loss. Shooting glasses, or any eye-glasses with hardened lenses, are also recommended for handgunners.

When you begin shooting at targets with a handgun, begin at a range of no more than 10 or 15 yards. Practice at this distance until you're regularly hitting the mark. Only then should you widen the distance between gun and target. You can tackle longer ranges if you'll use some kind of a rest, but when you're shooting offhand (standing) shooting at targets too distant too early only causes discouragement.

If you'll follow the safety rules and double check to make sure both the magazine and firing chamber(s) are unloaded, you can gain invaluable practice at home. Pick or make a mark high on a far wall, and practice keeping the sights lined up on the mark while you breathe, exhale, and s-q-u-e-e-z-e the trigger. Make sure there's no one on the far side of the wall, first (always be sure of your backstop, and where the bullet would go if the "empty" gun should somehow fire).

Periodically check to make sure the muzzle doesn't move when the hammer falls against the empty chamber. Any detectable movement means you flinched. Test yourself to see how long you can hold the sights steady on target.

Practicing on tin cans and other objects that bounce or fall over when hit is fun, but the sure test of marksmanship can be measured only on paper targets. When you can keep all your shots in the bullseye of a 25-yard pistol target at that distance shooting offhand, you're a fair handgun marksman. This mainly requires learned muscle control and determination.

CHAPTER 11

Handgun Sights

There are four basic types of handgun sights. The first are fixed sights not readily adjustable for windage or elevation. These sights consist of a front blade and a rear sighting notch or groove. Such rudimentary aiming aids are adequate for certain types of short-range shooting, and an experienced gunner can sometimes do surprisingly well at 25 or even 50 yards by learning to "hold off" the target to compensate for any built-in inaccuracies. Fixed sights lack the flexibility most sportsmen require.

The second, and by far the most popular type, is the target-style Patridge sight. This is an open, iron sight with an easily visible, square-top front blade and a micro-adjustable rear sight with a square-cornered U-shaped sighting notch. The square-faced sighting surfaces are easily visible by the shooter, and make precise alignment possible under most lighting conditions. Since these sights can be adjusted to move the bullet strike up and down or left and right on target, they can easily be adapted to different loads and ranges. While adjustable Patridge-style sights are taller and slightly wider than most fixed sights, they're very inconspicuous and add little bulk and almost no weight to the gun. They're also very fast to use.

The third style of handgun sight is the long eye relief scope. Unlike rifle scopes, which are held within 3 or 4 inches of the shooter's eye, handgun scopes are designed for use at arm's length. These scopes vary in magnification from 1½X to around 10X; most field gunners and hunters prefer relatively

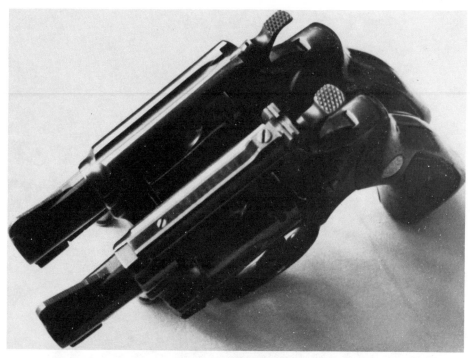

The handgun at top features fixed, nonadjustable sights. Note the simple sighting notch. The gun at bottom, however, has sights that can be moved.

The front blade of this Patridge-style sight features a flat, squared-off profile.

By far the most popular type of handgun sight is the target style Patridge sight. The rear sight is fully adjustable for both windage and elevation.

Long-eye-relief scopes are designed for handgun use. They're very popular on flat-shooting single-shots such as this Remington XP-100.

low-powered 2X or 4X models. The higher magnifications are for metallic silhouette target shooters and long-range varmint hunters.

Most handgun scopes feature crosshair reticles, and all are fully adjustable. Long eye relief scopes can be mounted on most revolvers, auto pistols and single shot handguns, although a certain amount of gunsmithing (drilling and tapping) may be required. Many single-shot pistols are used with magnifying scope sights, and most one-shooter models will accept scope mounts without drilling and tapping.

The fourth, and newest, type of handgun sight is the battery-powered electronic sight. The electronic sight projects a luminous red dot that appears in the reticle. The shooter simply places the dot over the intended target and squeezes the trigger.

Most electronic sights used on handguns are nonmagnifying. Since the target remains the same size, you can keep both eyes open. This gives you the full binocular effect, and makes the electronic sight extremely fast. You can find the target instantly and align the aiming dot almost as quickly.

Both scopes and electronic sights eliminate the need to keep three separate objects in near-simultaneous focus. Iron sights present the shooter with sight-

Electronic sights like the Swedish-built Aimpoint are becoming popular among handgunners. Such sights are extremely fast to use.

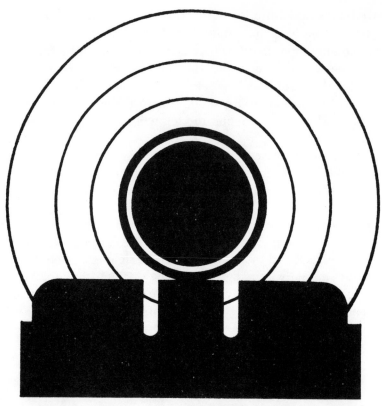

Most target gunners prefer the "6-o'clock" hold illustrated here. This simply means that the bullseye appears to sit atop the front sight at the six o'clock position.

ing elements set at three different distances from the eye. Because it's impossible to keep the rear sight, front sight and the target in sharp focus at the same time you must allow either the sights or the target to blur. Since the projected electronic dot and the scope's crosshair reticle appear in the same visual plane with the target, both target and sights can be kept in clear, sharp focus.

Most scopes present a magnified target image, and this can benefit the long-range shooter. On the other hand, electronic sights are faster, and lack parallax. Parallax is a condition in which the sighting reticle may be displaced in relation to the target as the eye moves to either side of the scope's centerline. In other words, if you don't position your eye exactly the same way behind the scope each time, a certain amount of aiming error will result. With electronic sights, this condition doesn't exist.

Both scopes and electronic sights add considerable bulk and weight to a handgun. As a result, special holsters are required for carrying guns fitted with these accessory sights. Some shooters simply attach slings to long-barreled scoped handguns, and carry them slung over one shoulder. These optical sights can also be expensive.

To aim with adjustable Patridge-style or nonadjustable fixed sights, look through the rear sighting notch and center the front sight blade in the notch. The top of the front sight blade should be exactly even with the shoulders of the rear sight. Finally, the top of the front sight blade should be in position so that it appears to bisect the target (for a "center hold") or so that the target seems to rest atop the front sight blade (the "6-o'clock hold"). Most target gunners prefer the latter ("6-o'clock hold") because the resulting "ball sitting on a post" sight picture doesn't require the shooter to bisect the bullseye with the sight blade. For shooting at circular bullseyes or other regularly shaped targets at known distances, the 6-o'clock hold offers some real advantages. Hunters of deer and other large game may prefer the center hold because it places the bullet exactly where the sight intersects the target—not several inches above that point.

Because it's impossible to keep both iron sights and target in simultaneous focus, you should concentrate on the *sights* and let the target blur. Keeping the front sight blade properly centered and level with top of the rear sighting notch is critical. A handgun has a relatively short sight radius (the distance between front and rear sights), and even a slight misalignment can throw the bullet way off course.

While handguns are theoretically sighted-in before they leave the factory, this isn't always true. Using different kinds of ammunition or different bullet weights also can significantly affect where the bullet strikes the target. This makes it necessary to sight your handgun in yourself to get decent accuracy.

If possible, do your shooting from a comfortable sitting position behind a sturdy bench rest. The handgun should be rested on sandbags to eliminate as much human error as possible. Use a steady, two-handed hold and an authoritative grip.

The initial sighting-in should be done with the target 25 yards downrange. If the bullets fail to impact anywhere on the target, move the target closer—say 10 or 12 yards. Move the rear sight in the direction you want the impact point to move on target. If the gun is shooting low and to the left, move the rear sights right and up. If the adjusting screws have no markings to indicate direction of movement, make a pencil mark on both sight base and blade to serve as a reference point. This will allow you to quickly determine which direction you must turn the windage screws to move the bullet strike right or left.

Once you have the sights adjusted so you're hitting the target dead center at

Handguns should be sighted-in from comfortable, sandbagged rest positions. Use a steady, two-handed hold to ensure better accuracy.

25 yards, you can either leave the sights at that setting or move the target to 50, 75, or 100 yards and repeat the process to sight in for longer range. Be sure to use the same load and bullet weight throughout. If you decide to change loads, you may have to readjust the sights to compensate for possible changes in the point of impact.

If your handgun shoots low and there's not sufficient elevation adjustment in the rear sight to raise the point of impact enough to bring the gun on target, you may have to reduce the height of the front sight by careful filing. Be sure to keep the top of the blade perfectly square and even. If the top slants even slightly, light reflecting from the surface can cause the sights to be misaligned. If you make any adjustments to the front sight, it should be moved in the *opposite* direction you want the bullet strike moved on target. Rear sights are moved in the *same* direction you want the bullet strike to move.

Sighting-in is simplified with electronic and scope sights. Both of these add-on sights feature micro-adjustable reticles, and the windage and elevation adjustment screws are clearly marked and calibrated.

CHAPTER 12

Begin With a Rimfire

Getting started on the right foot is even more important in handgunning than it is in rifle shooting. Handguns are more difficult to master, and if you don't learn the right habits from the beginning you may never learn to shoot a revolver or pistol well.

Some people buy a bigbore magnum as their first and only handgun. This is a mistake, particularly for a beginner. Even a relatively mild centerfire like a .38 Special or .380 ACP barks loudly enough and recoils sharply enough to be disconcerting. A 9mm Parabellum or .357 magnum bucks and bellows with even more authority, while a bigbore .45 or magnum .44 can really wallop a shooter's hands and eardrums.

Tackling a hard-kicking, ultra-noisy handgun right off the bat gives any new shooter a serious handicap. It may be possible to learn the basics of sight alignment, grip, stance, and trigger control with a powerful centerfire, but you'll first have to overcome your initial tendency to close both eyes, grimace, and jerk the trigger. When you begin with a bigbore handgun, the first thing you're almost guaranteed to learn is to flinch mightily every time you fire.

The ideal handgun to learn marksmanship skills with is the .22 rimfire. You can use an auto pistol, revolver, or single shot, as long as it's chambered for the soft-spoken .22. The cartridge of choice is the .22 long rifle—*not* the more potent (and more costly) .22 WMR, or magnum.

Even the .22 rimfire can be noisy in a short-barreled handgun, but it's

Rimfire ammo offers fine accuracy even in short-barreled .22's. It's recommended, however, that you buy a handgun with a barrel length of six or eight inches for most sporting uses.

guaranteed to be easier on your ears than any centerfire you can name. As far as recoil is concerned, the .22's kick is practically nonexistent. Rimfire handguns are relatively inexpensive, and .22 ammunition is downright cheap. This means you can afford to practice long and regularly when you shoot a .22 rimfire. You don't even need to bother saving the empty cartridge casings, as they can't be reloaded anyhow.

Finally, many .22 handguns are exceptionally accurate. The .22 long rifle cartridge has a deserved reputation as a real tack driver, and most pistols and revolvers chambered for the round shoot exactly where you point them. If you miss, you can generally be sure it's not the fault of the gun or its ammunition.

There are dozens of different .22 handguns on the market. In fact there are

Here's a bull-barreled handgun with adjustable sights. It's a .22 made by Harrington & Richardson.

so many that narrowing the choice down can be a problem if you don't know what to look for. Most of the rimfire revolvers and auto pistols now being sold will give good service and offer excellent value, but there are certain things you should look for.

As I pointed out in chapter 11, fixed sights offer certain utility, but a good set of fully adjustable, Patridge-style target sights are a real plus on any handgun. If a fixed-sight gun doesn't shoot to point of aim, there's only so much you can do about it. You can file down the front sight blade to make the gun shoot higher, and it may be possible to drift either the front or rear sight sideways in its dovetail. But if those solutions fail to do the trick, about all you can do is learn to shoot high, low, or to one side to compensate for improperly regulated sights. If you're serious about becoming an expert shot with a handgun, select one with easily visible, adjustable sights.

Trigger pull is also important. Some low-priced .22 revolvers have double-action triggers that are so stiff and heavy, decent accuracy is next to impossible. While a poor double-action pull is forgiveable, a handgun that displays a too-heavy single-action trigger is a more serious problem. If the trigger action is stubbornly stiff after the gun is cocked, you'll have a hard time hitting what you shoot at. Many triggers can be made much smoother by a little competent gunsmithing (don't attempt this yourself unless you have the necessary know-how); others are of poor design and can't be greatly improved.

So the second thing to look for is a good, crisp single-action trigger that isn't too heavy. This is a desirable feature for any revolver or auto pistol you may be considering.

Test the action. Does the gun function smoothly, or does it appear to be mechanically ragged? If you're buying a used .22 handgun, be sure to insist on firing the gun at the nearest range to see how well it functions. This is particularly important for autoloaders; if the gun doesn't feed and fire reliably with a variety of both high-speed and standard-velocity .22 long rifle ammunition, pass it by. If a revolver is out of time, it may spit quantities of lead sideways from the gap between barrel and cylinder. A small amount of spitting can be considered normal, but if the gun spatters annoyingly reject it. If a new gun exhibits these characteristics when you first shoot it, return it to the dealer.

Don't buy a handgun with a too-short barrel. Snubnosed revolvers and auto pistols are designed for concealability and self-defense; they're not target guns. Buy a gun with a barrel at least 4 inches long, and for serious target work 5, 6 or 8 inches is better.

Check the balance, and see how the gun feels in your hand. Does the gun seem to point naturally, or does it feel awkward? A certain amount of muzzle heaviness is desirable, as the extra weight out front can help steady your aim. Accessory grips can often be added to the gun to improve its feel and controllability.

Rimfire handguns come in a variety of barrel lengths. For serious target work, long barrels are best.

Most target shooters prefer auto pistols, and there are a number of excellent .22 target guns on the market. At the same time many rimfire revolvers are capable of fine accuracy. A quality handgun of either type will give very good service.

It's a good idea to buy the best you can afford when purchasing a handgun. If you amortize the price over the lifetime of service you can expect from a quality pistol or revolver, the per-year cost becomes negligible. But there are some bargains worth mentioning. One of the best .22 handgun values on the market is Ruger's Mark II Target Model—a very reasonably priced .22 auto pistol with excellent, adjustable sights. The Standard Model Mark II is even more affordable, but lacks adjustable sights. The Target Model is well worth the slight difference in price.

High Standard, Harrington & Richardson, Colt, Ruger, Smith & Wesson, Charter Arms, Browning, Dan Wesson, Interarms, Stoeger, and others all make good, serviceable .22 rimfire revolvers and auto pistols suitable for

Ruger's Mark II Target Model is an outstanding value in a .22 auto pistol. It features excellent design, adjustable target sights, and fine mechanical workmanship.

Rimfire handguns can be used on a variety of plinking targets and provide very low-cost shooting practice.

beginners and experts alike. Since you want to become an expert, it only makes sense to buy as much quality as you can afford. A good, well-balanced handgun with a smooth, acceptably light trigger and adjustable target sights will make the road to "expert" status both shorter and less bumpy.

Once you've selected the right rimfire handgun, practice with it often. Shoot at both printed paper targets and tin cans. Try to decrease the size of your groups on paper each week—work on holding the muzzle (and sights) steady on target, and constantly strive to perfect your trigger control. Plinking at tin cans and other informal targets won't give you the same empirical feedback, but it provides fun, valuable practice.

Shoot from a rest now and then, and try the four basic stances: offhand, kneeling, sitting, and prone. Vary your range, and try a variety of targets. Rimfire-scale metallic silhouette targets are both fun and challenging to a rimfire handgunner.

While .22 handguns are far less noisy than their centerfire cousins, a short-barreled pistol or revolver can produce enough decibels to cause permanent hearing damage. You'll be more comfortable—and shoot better—if you wear adequate ear protection. Shooting glasses are also a good idea.

CHAPTER 13

How to Shoot a Bigbore Handgun Well

Moving up to a centerfire handgun needn't be traumatic. The shooting skills learned with a mild-mannered .22 are fully transferable to the heaviest magnum. A booming bigbore may buck and bellow, but there's no need to be intimidated by noise and recoil.

Some shooters are intimidated by big, magnum handguns. The real problem isn't noise and recoil—they're easily controlled. The problem of shooting a large centerfire handgun well is largely psychological. If you're afraid of the gun, there's no way you're going to become a decent marksman with it. It's important to have the right mental attitude.

For example, I acquired a Ruger Super Blackhawk .44 magnum revolver when my youngest son was 9 years old. The .44 magnum has long had a reputation for producing fearsome recoil; it was and remains the most potent revolver cartridge on the market.

My son accompanied me to the range to give the new gun a workout, and insisted on shooting it. I was a bit hesitant because my son was recovering from surgery on his right hand. I wasn't sure it was sufficiently healed to let him control the big magnum. Nonetheless, he talked me into it. He'd fired a number of other handguns, including some smaller magnums. I always insisted he wear good ear protection, and I'd taught him to grip guns firmly in

This young shooter has the right idea: Get the ear protection on first, especially when shooting big-bore handguns.

both hands and to be prepared for recoil. He took the big .44 in stride, and nearly shot up all my expensive ammo before I could get the gun away from him that day. He paid little attention to the jolt and less to the noise, and simply found shooting the magnum a whole lot of fun.

While we were taking turns shooting the Super Blackhawk, another gunner walked over to examine it. He was a large man—over six feet tall, and nudging 200 pounds. When I offered to let him shoot the .44 magnum, he threw up his hands in horror. "Not me!" he said, backing away. "I've heard all about that caliber. You won't catch *me* shooting a gun that kicks that hard!"

When I pointed out that my young son had been shooting it with great enjoyment in spite of an injured hand, the man looked at us as if we were both crazy, and walked away shaking his head.

The point is, any handgun *is* controllable—and by almost anyone old enough to be entrusted to shoot one by himself (or herself). Recoil is nothing more than the gun pushing back toward the shooter. It can be a fairly sharp push, but it's not really punishing. You can hit your shooting hand a lot harder by simply striking the open palm with your other fist. Strangely, people who don't find that activity threatening may be scared to death to shoot a handgun that recoils with much less force.

Recoil from the largest magnum is nothing more than the gun pushing back toward the shooter. It's not painful or punishing. Ear protection helps prevent recoil fear by reducing noise.

One reason some shooters find centerfire handguns intimidating is the loud noise these guns produce. The combination of recoil and muzzle blast can be disconcerting. This is why adequate ear protection is so important whenever you fire a centerfire handgun. A good, muff-type protector that fits over each ear and seals out sound effectively muffles the loudest muzzle blast to a mild "pop." Once you eliminate the jarring noise that can painfully assault the eardrums, the battle is half won. Any bigbore seems to kick substantually less when muzzle blast is deadened. If you doubt this, try firing a magnum handgun while wearing adequate ear protection, then remove the earmuffs or plugs and fire the same gun again. You'll swear it recoils a lot harder when your ears are unprotected.

The next step is to grip the gun firmly in both hands, as outlined in chapter 10. You needn't squeeze until your knuckles turn white; simply grip the gun with authority. The shooting hand should be positioned as high as comfortably possible on the grip, with the supporting hand wrapped around the fingers of the shooting hand. Wrists and elbows should be locked, and you should lean slightly forward into the gun as you fire.

With their smoothly rounded "plow-handle" grips, Western-style single-action revolvers translate much of the recoil into an easy-to-control rotating motion.

When the gun recoils, allow your body to move with the recoil force. A Western-styled single-action sixgun with its characteristic "plow-handle" grips will tend to rotate in your hand as the barrel whips up and back. This will cause your hands and arms to raise. Because of this rotating motion, many shooters find the recoil of Western-styled single-action revolvers milder and more controllable than the kick of other handguns.

Auto pistols, double-action revolvers and single-shot handguns tend to recoil directly back into the shooter's hands. A firm grip is particularly important here, and the arms and body should be allowed to move back with recoil. Again, the arms will rise as they pivot from the shoulders.

Don't hold your body rigid; let it move in response to the recoil. Allow the entire body to absorb the gun's "kick;" it's a mistake to let your hands take all the punishment.

Some magnum revolvers have sharply checkered grips that can cut and abrade the hands. Either replace these grips with more comfortable accessory grips, or wear leather gloves when you shoot. Pachmayr and other suppliers

Use a firm, two-handed hold such as this and you can learn to shoot any magnum handgun well.

make soft neoprene replacement grips that can go a long way toward taming the effects of recoil.

Once you've fired several rounds through your centerfire revolver or auto-loader, let someone else load the gun while you look away. If the gun is a revolver, your coach should load only 3 or 4 chambers at random, and leave the other chambers empty. If you're shooting an autoloader, have your coach single load the rounds and leave the firing chamber empty every now and then. You won't know whether the gun will fire or not as you pull the trigger. If you've developed an accuracy-destroying flinch, it will quickly show up as the hammer falls on an empty chamber.

This kind of practice helps you develop discipline, and makes sure the muzzle remains steady each and every time you shoot. Dry firing with the chamber empty helps promote steadiness, but you must learn to maintain the same rock-steady hold with live ammo on the firing range.

Let someone else load your magnum revolver, leaving some chambers empty. You shouldn't flinch when the hammer falls on an unloaded chamber.

The problems encountered in controlling a bigbore handgun are primarily psychological. Once you become convinced that the gun can be controlled without superhuman effort, you can go about the business of improving your marksmanship skills.

CHAPTER 14

Recognizing Range Limitations

While some scoped handguns are capable of killing game cleanly or printing golf ball-sized groups at 200 yards or more, few sportsmen are skillful enough to take full advantage of this potential.

Shooting at metallic silhouettes, tin cans, or paper targets at extreme ranges is harmless, if frustrating fun. It's possible to become reasonably deadly with a handgun at surprising distances, but this takes both time and practice. It also takes fairly specialized firearms and sights. Metallic silhouette handgunners regularly topple targets at 200 meters, but not the first time they try it.

The point is, target shooters and gunners who plink at inanimate objects can well afford to shoot at barrel-stretching ranges. Even if they lack the expertise to hit what they shoot at, there's no harm done. The worst they can do is waste ammunition.

Hunters must abide by an entirely different set of rules. They should avoid attempting shots at live game unless they're more than reasonably sure of placing their shots accurately in the kill zone. Simply hitting an animal isn't enough—the bullet must be properly placed to ensure a quick, humane death.

That means you must learn your range limitations, and take care not to exceed them in the hunting field. If you're an expert shot armed with a flat-shooting, single-shot pistol mated with a good scope, you may be fully justified in shooting at a deer or antelope at 200 yards. Even then, you should make sure you're in good shooting position and have a steady rest.

Many shooters limit their shooting to ranges of 50 or 60 yards when hunting deer-sized game. Even though they're excellent marksmen, they realize their open-sighted .357 or .44 magnum revolvers make sure kills problematical at much longer distances. Much of the challenge—and rewards—of handgun hunting lies not in testing your long-range shooting skills, but in your ability to stalk within sure pistol range.

Because gunning skills differ widely, every shooter must determine his practical range limitations before attempting to hunt with a handgun. The only way to do this is to try shooting at targets set at various distances. Do your best to simulate field conditions. Shoot from the offhand, sitting, or kneeling position, and get your shots away quickly, as if the target was a deer that could turn and bolt any second. Shoot at least three shots in rapid succession at each target.

When you can keep three consecutive shots on a 9-inch paper plate, not just

Expert marksmen armed with a flat-shooting pistol and shooting from a very steady position can justifiably take game at 200 yards or more.

For any other than point-blank range, which is rare in hunting, always find the steadiest possible shooting position.

As a general rule of thumb, if you can keep your shots on a 9-inch plate at a given distance from field positions, you can justify shooting at a deer at that range.

once but every time you try it, you can justify shooting at deer-sized game at that distance. Determine your effective range from all shooting stances. You may find you can hit the paper plate every time at 80 yards (or paces) from the sitting position, but have to cut the range to 40 yards to have similar success shooting offhand. That means you shouldn't try to down a deer at 60 yards unless you have time to drop to a sitting position or take advantage of some natural rest.

While your own marksmanship abilities are a definite limiting factor, your choice of gun and cartridge also enter in. Some cartridges have a rainbow trajectory, while others shoot very flat. Accuracy is difficult beyond the 100-yard mark unless you know exactly how far the bullet you're shooting drops at 120, 140, or 150 yards.

Some scope-sighted guns are chambered for very high-velocity rifle rounds, and can be used to take varmints at ranges beyond 200 yards. Since the target is a rodent-sized animal only a few inches square, a high-speed bullet will usually either kill instantly or miss clean. In this case, long-range attempts can do little harm.

Shooting at deer, antelope, or similar game at very long range with a handgun is another matter entirely. A near miss will only wound the animal. A properly equipped expert who really knows how to shoot might be justified in shooting at a deer 150 yards distant. But for the vast majority of us, hunting deer-sized game with a handgun is definitely a short-range proposition.

Most handgunning hunters I know will pass up shots beyond 75 yards when armed with an open-sighted revolver. Scope sights make precise bullet placement easier, and can stretch the effective range several yards. In the final analysis, only you know how well you can shoot. Use the "paper plate" test, and rank yourself accordingly. When you do shoot at live game afield, be sure to assume your steadiest position and take full advantage of any natural rest close at hand. Take a deep breath, say a short prayer to ward off "buck fever," and carefully squeeze the trigger.

While the majority of handguns and gunners do their best work at ranges this side of 100 yards, some hybrid guns have the accuracy potential of rifles at surprising distance. Scoped, single-shot pistols chambered for high-intensity rifle cartridges like the .308 Winchester and other flat-shooting rounds are intended specifically for long-range work. Freestyle metallic silhouette target shooters adopt a modified Creedmore position, lying on their back with the pistol steadied against an upraised leg, and can hit small marks consistently well beyond 200 meters. In these kind of experienced hands, a pistol becomes as accurate as a rifle, with roughly the same practical range.

The keys to successful long-range handgunning are judgement, and skills

Whenever you shoot at live game, be sure to take advantage of any available rest to give you the best chance for steady shooting. Note how the shooter buffers contact between the tree and gun with his hands.

gained through diligent practice. Know your equipment and its abilities. Most handgun hunting cartridges are suitable out to 50 or 75 yards, and the most experienced expert won't attempt to use them on game much beyond that distance. Unless you have a handgun and sights specifically designed for long-range shooting, and you're confident of your ability to keep your shots in the sure kill range of a target animal at that distance, pass up the long shots and try to stalk closer.

CHAPTER 15

Handgunning Target Sports

Competitve handgunners fall into several categories. There are the formal paper punchers who shoot at paper bullseyes in accordance with both national and international rules. Police officers and civilians alike participate in stylized matches designed to simulate combat conditions. A growing number of handgunners spend several weekends each year shooting at life-sized metallic cutouts of chickens, turkeys, pigs, and sheep.

In addition, there are even less orthodox "fun" events that yearly attract their share of competitors. As an example, there's the Second Chance Bowling Pin Shoot in which bigbore handgunners race the clock to see who can knock five bowling pins from a table in the least amount of time.

Turkey shoots are held all across the country each fall. This is a sport that originated with riflemen, but many handgunning organizations have adopted the format. Shooters pay a fee for each shot fired, with a small, difficult mark used as the target. Contestants fire in turn, and the first gunner to hit the target takes home the prize—usually a live or freshly butchered turkey. This kind of event is often used as a club fundraiser, and several turkeys will be offered during an afternoon shoot.

The National Rifle Associaton (NRA), with its affiliated local clubs, sponsors and promotes a variety of competitive handgun shoots nationwide. These include the famed NRA National Championship and National Trophy matches held each year at Camp Perry, Ohio.

The Camp Perry matches are open to any NRA member, but typically draw only top-seeded shooters. NRA National Match Course events are also held by local gun clubs all across the country, and these meets attract tyros and more experienced shooters alike.

Standard National Match Course competition consists of two 5-round strings with 10 seconds allotted for each string (rapid fire), an additional pair of 5-round strings at 20 seconds per string (timed fire), and 10 rounds timed at a full minute per round (slow fire). Slow fire is conducted at a range of 50 yards, while the other segments of the shoot are fired at 25 yards. A short version of the course utilizes a 25-yard range for all three types of fire.

A .45-caliber auto pistol is required in National Match Course competition. The Colt Gold Cup shown here is a favorite among serious shooters.

The full National Match Pistol Course can be fired by using only two handguns, a
.22 rimfire and .45 auto. This target case holds all the shooter needs for the
competition. (Courtesy of National Rifle Association)

The NRA National Match Course is fired from the one-handed standing position.
See how the shooter, although holding the gun steady and bracing himself, appears
completely relaxed.

Three different handguns are used to fire the National Match Course. A .22 pistol or revolver having a barrel length of not more than 10 inches (including cylinder) is used for the rimfire segment. A centerfire handgun of .32 or larger caliber is used to shoot the centerfire course. Again, maximum barrel length is 10 inches. The third part of the competition can be shot only with a .45-caliber semi-automatic pistol. The distance between front and rear sights can't exceed 10 inches for any handgun used in National Match Course competion.

While the rules allow the use of revolvers in the rimfire and centerfire segments, most competitors rely on auto pistols. Auto pistols needn't be manually cocked between shots to obtain a single-action trigger pull, and this saves valuable time when you're shooting against the clock. Auto pistols as a rule offer more consistent accuracy than revolvers deliver.

The official NRA National Match Course target features a bullseye measuring 3.39 inches across. The bullseye contains a 1.695-inch X-ring, which is used to settle ties. A shot in the bullseye counts 10 points. The 9-ring is 5.54 inches in diameter, while the next larger ring (which adds 8 points to the score) measures 8 inches across. The large outside ring is 19.68 inches in diameter; a hit here counts 5 points. Shots outside this ring are scored as a miss.

The NRA National Match course is fired from the formal one-handed standing target position. There are 300 points possible with each type of gun, which means a full 3-gun course of fire yields a possible 900 points.

International handgun competition can be even more demanding. The scoring rings are smaller and shooting is done at longer range. A variety of international handgun shoots are held in this country and abroad, and competition extends to the Olympic Games.

Free pistol shooting is a highly specialized European sport that has received little attention in this country. Unorthodox .22 rimfire handguns are used, as "free pistol" design is relatively free of restrictions. Some free pistols fire with only a half ounce of trigger pressure.

International Rapid Fire competition also uses fairly specialized handguns. This sport is so fast-paced that most shooters use finely tuned guns chambered for the low-recoiling .22 Short cartridge. Recovering from the minimal recoil of a .22 Long Rifle round takes up too much time.

There are other international handgun sports that are more closely related to American forms of competition. These include the International Center Fire and Standard Pistol shoots. Unfortunately, most American handgunning organizations are very parochial, and international-type matches are rare in this country.

In contrast, another type of shooting competition that originated in another country has taken American handgunners by storm. Metallic silhouette was born in Mexico as entertainment at local fiestas. American shooters in Southwest border states adopted the sport, and it has since become our fastest-growing form of handgun competition. Riflemen have their own version.

Metallic silhouette uses life-sized steel cutouts of chickens, javelinas, turkeys, and rams set at ranges of 50, 100, 150, and 200 meters. The targets stand on small steel bases, and clang loudly when hit by a centerfire handgun bullet. Unless struck squarely, the target may spin or simply wobble. The silhouette must fall over on its side to count as a hit. Because hits can be readily seen and heard by competitors and spectators alike, this animated sport is more fun for everyone involved. Punching holes in paper lacks the spectator interest that metallic silhouettes generate.

Rimfire silhouette is similar, except the targets are scaled down and shot at half the distances used in the centerfire sport. Of course, only .22 rimfire handguns are allowed.

Metallic silhouette matches are governed by either the National Rifle Association (NRA) or the International Handgun Metallic Silhouette Association (IHMSA) rules. Information about IHMSA shoots and local organizations can be obtained by writing IHMSA, Box 1609, Idaho Falls, Idaho 83401. For

Metallic silhouette competition features life-size steel cutouts of animals set from 50 to 200 meters away. Notice that even those not in the act of shooting are wearing ear protection. And look how small those targets appear. (Courtesy of National Rifle Association)

Metallic silhouette freestyle shooting allows virtually any position that doesn't give the handgun artificial support. This shooter may look uncomfortable, but take a closer look and you'll see that the gun is very well balanced and supported. (Courtesy of National Rifle Association)

Competing with other fine shooters helps you hone your marksmanship skills. (Courtesy of National Rifle Association)

information regarding any type of NRA handgunning, contact the National Rifle Association, 1600 Rhode Island Avenue, N.W., Washington, D.C. 20036.

If you'd like to try your hand at the unorthodox "knock the bowling pin off the table" competition mentioned earlier, contact the sponsor: Second Chance Body Armor, Inc., P.O. Box 578, Central Lake, Michigan 49622.

The Yellow Pages of your telephone book may yield the address and phone number of a local gun club, or you can inquire at your neighborhood gun shop or sporting goods store for information about organized pistol competition.

Shooting competitively helps you become an expert shot. Nothing builds concentration faster than comparing your ability with other experienced shooters. You can also learn a lot by watching the style and stance of top-scoring competitors. Most will be willing to offer a few minutes' coaching, if asked politely *after* the match has ended. The pointers you pick up can be invaluable.

CHAPTER 16

Hunting With a Handgun

Handgun hunters fall into two basic categories: those who hunt deer and other large game, and those who restrict their handgunning to prairie dogs, squirrels, rabbits and other small game.

Handguns have been used to kill all manner of game, up to and including elephant. That doesn't mean handguns are really suitable for hunting large, dangerous game. Even expert marksmen using specialized hybrid handguns that have the potency of a magnum rifle take care to have an experienced rifleman back them up. If you insist on tackling large, pugnacious beasts like Alaskan grizzlies with a handgun providing your sole firepower, you're asking for trouble. Such animals can absorb a lot of punishment and remain in action—and they're perfectly capable of "shooting back."

While some custom-made or semi-custom single shot pistols chamber surprisingly potent cartridges, most production handguns digest much milder loads than rifles are capable of handling. The Thompson/Center Contender is a single-shot pistol offered in a wide variety of chamberings, including the .35 Remington, .30-30 Winchester, .223 Remington, and other rifle rounds. These cartridges aren't particularly powerful when fired from a rifle, and are even less potent from the Contender's shorter barrel.

Similarly, the .44 magnum has long held the title of the world's most powerful revolver cartridge, yet it generates no more energy than the .30-30

Hunting small game with a handgun adds challenge to already challenging sport. You have the responsibility, however, to choose a caliber equal to the task—one that has the ability to kill your quarry cleanly.

Winchester—a carbine load some modern deer hunters scorn as under-powered. No experienced big-game hunter would seriously think of using a .30-30 carbine on grizzly. Yet a surprising number of handgunners seem eager to tackle this same, dangerous critter with their pet .44's. Such optimism is best discouraged.

At the same time, certain handguns and cartridges are suitable for hunting deer and other large game. Where handguns are permitted for hunting deer, guns shooting .357 Maximum, .357 magnum, .41 magnum, or .44 magnum cartridges are often specified. Most experts agree that the .357 magnum is only marginal for deer-sized game, and this is certainly the lower practical limit as far as power is concerned.

What handguns are suitable for hunting deer-sized game? Any good double-action or single-action revolver chambered for the just-mentioned cartridges are a good choice, as long as you know how to shoot it and limit the

Long-barreled magnums are ideal for hunting deer-sized game. Most hunters should limit their handgun shots to 75 yards or less.

range to under 75 yards. Ideally, the gun should have adjustable sights and a barrel at least 6 inches long. With a long eye-relief 2X or 4X scope you might be able to extend the range a few yards, but revolver cartridges aren't flat-shooting or potent enough for work much beyond 100 yards. An autoloader chambered for the .45 Winchester Magnum will also do the job.

A single-shot pistol with an 8, 10 or 14-inch barrel makes a fine handgun for hunting deer-sized (and larger) game, provided it's chambered for a sufficiently potent round. The recommended list includes the .308 Winchester (available in certain bolt-action single shots), the wildcat 6.5mm, and 7mm Thompson/Center-Ugalde, the .30 and .357 Herrett, .35 Remington, .30-30 Winchester and the .357, .41, and .44 magnum rounds mentioned earlier. While the .357 magnum is considered marginal on deer, the newer, longer .357 Maximum makes an excellent hunting load.

Small-game hunters use rimfire and centerfire handguns alike, but adjust their shooting range to the cartridge limitation. For varmints at 150 yards and

Rimfire .22 handguns shouldn't be used for game much larger than rabbits. And if you can do well with bouncing game like this, hunting deer-sized animals will present little extra challenge.

beyond they rely on scoped centerfires chambered for such flat-shooting rounds as the .22 Hornet, .221 Fireball, and .223 Remington. These are available only in single-shot pistols.

The .357 magnum, .357 Maximum, and similar revolver rounds shoot flat enough to kill regularly to 125 yards or so, while numbers like the .38 Special, 9mm Parabellum, and .32 magnum are 100-yard propositions. In a scoped handgun, the .22 Long Rifle and .22 WMR rimfires can be used to take small game at 100 yards. If you use iron sights, the rimfire .22's should be limited to 50 or 60 yards for best results. The rimfire .22's shouldn't be used for game much larger than rabbits and squirrels, even though they're capable of killing foxes, coyotes, and even cougar under the right circumstances.

The ranges just mentioned should be considered maximum ranges. Even in the hands of top-flight experts, these cartridges simply aren't up to performing well farther out. When you elect to hunt game with a handgun, you must realize that means passing up many shots a rifleman would take. The handgun is basically a short-range shooting tool, and one of the attractions of limiting the effective range of your armament is the necessity to stalk close to your quarry.

Because the handgun is also more difficult than a rifle to master, you're accepting the additional challenge of becoming highly proficient with your revolver or pistol before carrying it afield. Because handguns are typically less powerful than centerfire hunting rifles, shot placement is even more important. There's no power margin to spare, and you must hit a vital mark exactly for a clean kill.

Because handguns used for hunting have relatively long barrels and may be fitted with a bulky scope or electronic sight, the traditional belt holster doesn't work well in the game field. Drawing a 7½- or 8-inch barreled gun from a belt holster becomes very awkward, and toting 4 or 5 pounds of scoped magnum at your hip puts you off balance.

For long-barreled, heavy hunting handguns, a shoulder holster is the best answer. A shoulder holster keeps the gun high on the chest or under your arm where it's out of the way. The gun is also very accessible. Shoulder holsters are available for scoped and iron-sighted handguns alike, and can be worn over your outer clothing.

Belt-mounted holsters are practical only if your hunting handgun has a barrel 6 inches or less in length, and wears open iron sights. Even then, you should avoid the heavy buscadero "Western gunfighter" rigs. Choose a light, sturdy holster that carries the gun high over the hip. Ideally, the holster will have a snap-fastened security strap to keep the gun in place until it's ready for use.

As I've pointed out in preceding chapters, expert handgunners take every possible advantage when hunting game. They stalk as closely as possible, and make use of any available natural rest. They seldom shoot from the unsteady standing position. If there's time, they'll drop to the sitting or prone stance, and steady their shooting hand against a tree stump or boulder.

Hunting handgunners almost never fire double action. They'll cock their guns before each shot, and take careful aim before squeezing the trigger. But above all, they'll start to practice months before the hunt. They know there's no substitute for marksmanship, and no real sportsman will carry a handgun in the hunting field until he's confident he can place his shots precisely on targets that are in range. And he won't exceed that range.

Practicing on metallic game silhouettes placed at varying distances is an excellent way of improving your chances in the game field. The small-scale rimfire targets are particularly good for small game hunters, although any diminutive mark can be used to improve your shooting skills. Plinking at tin cans is both relaxing and beneficial.

Actually, one of the best ways to prepare for hunting deer or other large

Hunting handgunners seldom use the unsteady standing position if there's time to drop to a more stable stance, such as this sitting position.

One of the best ways to prepare to hunt deer with a handgun is to sharpen your eye on game such as fast-stepping jackrabbits. It's a lot of fun, too.

game with a bigbore handgun is to hunt smaller game with the same firearm. Jackrabbits provide both lively and plentiful targets in most parts of the country, and can usually be hunted year around. If you can hit a bouncing jack at 40 or 50 yards with your big .44, you won't have any trouble duplicating the feat on a trophy buck when deer season rolls around.

There's no substitute for time spent in the hunting field. Carry a rimfire revolver or auto pistol whenever you hike through the woods. If no small game is in season, practice plinking at fallen twigs, driftwood, or other expendable litter. Never deface private property by shooting at it, and always be sure you have a safe backstop.

Constant practice is required if you wish to become an expert handgunner—and only experts should consider hunting deer or other game with a revolver or pistol.

CHAPTER 17

Shotgunning Basics: How to Hit a Moving Target

Some self-taught scattergunners seem to have an inherent knack for the sport. The right instincts, balance, and coordination are already in place, and these fortunate individuals have no trouble shooting a shotgun well practically from the first moment they pick one up.

Relatively few first-time shooters are this talented. Most of us who learned how to hit moving objects with a shotgun through trial-and-error tribulation have had varying degrees of success. If we got started on the wrong foot—and many of us did—we were lucky to eventually become mediocre wing shots. The rare, natural experts had to overcome an assortment of bad habits picked up along the way.

The first step to becoming an expert shot with a scattergun is to learn the right instincts and habits. People who begin their firearms education with a rifle or handgun often have trouble mastering the scattergun. Rifles and handguns are precisely aimed at the target using a variety of precision sighting instruments. The rifle itself is all but forgotten as the shooter concentrates on the sights and their relationship to the target.

A good shotgunner doesn't use any kind of mechanical, adjustable, or

When shooting a shotgun, concentrate on the target, not the barrel or front sight. Instinctive shooting is deadly on game, and the ability to shoot well makes scenes like this all the more memorable and enjoyable.

optical sights. Shotguns come equipped with a round, front bead, but even this rudimentary sighting aid isn't needed and should be ignored. The eye may be subliminally aware of the sighting rib and front bead, but the vast majority of experts won't even be conscious of these objects in his vision.

A truly good scattergunner learns to position his eye at just the right point behind the barrel. The cheek is positioned firmly on the buttstock's comb, and the gun is held so that it becomes an extension of the body. The head should be held straight, not craned awkwardly forward or to either side. This is critical. In effect, the eye is the shotgun's sight. If it's improperly positioned, the gun will shoot high, low, or to one side. Learn to position the head properly on the stock each and every time, and the eye will always be in the right place. Your "sights" will be correctly adjusted.

Once the head and eye are in the right place behind the gun, you should practice moving the head, gun, and eye together. Learn to move your whole

The ability to hit fast-moving targets that appear by surprise is important to the upland hunter.

upper body from the hips when you look at a target. The relationship between the head, eye, and gun should remain the same. When your eye tracks a moving target, the gun should automatically follow.

While a rifle and handgun are carefully aimed, you must shoot a shotgun instinctively. Learn to concentrate on the *target*—not the gun or front sighting bead.

Strangely enough, learning the right instincts is best done not with a shotgun, but with an inexpensive BB gun. The U.S. Army once used BB guns to teach instinctive "quick-kill" shooting; the method was fast, inexpensive, and highly effective. In his excellent book, "Shotgunning: The Art and the Science" (Winchester Press), my friend Bob Brister told of teaching a teenaged girl how to shoot well in less than a week with his own version of the method. He had her practice with a BB gun a half hour twice daily for seven days. Then he took her to the local skeet range and placed a shotgun in her hands. She began breaking targets almost immediately.

Both beginners and experienced shooters alike can benefit from the same basic regimen. Tyros will learn to shoot properly from the beginning, while older hands can unlearn some bad habits through a week of daily BB gun practice:

Before you begin, there's one other chore you should take care of. You need to learn which is your "master eye." As you may know, your two eyes aren't equal partners in the viewing game. One of the pair is always dominant. If you shoot right-handed and your right is dominant, well and good. But if you're right-handed and have a left "master eye," you have a problem that must be resolved before you can hope to become a decent scattergun shot.

It's easy to learn which is your master eye. Simply cut a hole 2 or 3 inches wide in the center of a piece of type or notebook paper. Pick out a distant object. Then hold the paper a foot or so in front of your eyes and look at the object through the hole, all the while keeping both eyes open. Next, shut your left eye. If the object remains in view, your right eye is dominant. If the object disappears, the left eye is the master one.

If you're right-handed, hopefully the right eye will be dominant. Southpaws are best served by left master eyes. If neither situation is the case, you would be well advised to learn to shoot from the shoulder directly below your dominant eye. This may seem awkward at first, but it's the best and easiest solution.

Gunners who shoot right-handed despite a left master eye are likely to cross-shoot the target. In other words, the shot pattern will center off to one side. Squinting the off eye can help relieve the problem, and is the solution often used. Other gunners have expensive offset stocks custom made to place the dominant eye in line with the barrel. Still others attempt to mechanically block or impair the vision of the stronger eye while they're shooting. This can be done by smearing a small dab of oil, wax, or petroleum jelly on one lens of your shooting glasses. The dab should be carefully positioned over the offending eye while you look down the gun barrel with the firearm held in shooting position. A small smear in the right place will partially blot out the end of the barrel for one eye, while the eye behind the gun retains a clear view of the muzzle.

Once you've resolved the "master eye" problem by one means or another (if such a problem exists), you're ready to begin. You'll need an inexpensive BB gun and some small, easily seen targets. Ping pong balls work fine, but the tiniest paper cups or printed bullseyes serve equally well.

Buy a supply of BB's, then remove the sights from your BB gun. Leave neither front nor rear sight in place. Instinctive shooting requires a completely bare barrel. Retire to your back yard or anywhere else you can shoot BB's safely. Make sure you have a high fence or some other suitable backstop to arrest ricochets.

Place several targets in the grass 15 or 20 feet away. Lower the BB gun from your shoulder, and quickly choose a target at random. Immediately shoulder the gun while you concentrate on the target—*not* on the gun. Then pull the trigger.

It's important to develop the right stance and habits from the beginning. Make sure your head is straight and upright, not craned down to meet the stock. Bend forward slightly into the gun, and move from the waist when you swing on target. Your head and eye must maintain the same relationship with the gun at all times.

Shoot at least a half hour each day, and keep practicing for a week or more. Leave your shotgun alone in the meantime. Remember to concentrate on the target, and pay the BB gun itself as little attention as possible. Periodically check yourself to make sure your head is properly positioned on the stock and that your eye is in the right place.

You'll undoubtedly miss a lot at first. Then your eye will begin registering the pellet strikes, and you'll automatically start compensating to bring the impact on target. Don't consciously try to line up the gun barrel with the target; let your instincts take over. You'll soon find those BB's are coming closer to the mark. Before long you'll be hitting those tiny targets regularly with almost every shot.

Work on your body stance while all this is going on. If you shoot right handed, your left foot should be slightly forward. Practice moving your entire body with the gun, never just the gun alone. If the gun changes position in relation to your head and eye, you'll miss. Adjust your shooting stance until it feels natural and you're comfortably balanced. Always make sure you lean into, not away from the gun.

There's always the danger you'll begin unconsciously positioning your head improperly on the stock. If you fall into this "wrong way" habit, your brain may compensate until you're hitting the targets once again. But you'll never become a really good shot with your head in an awkward position. It can be helpful to have another shooter coach you periodically to make sure you don't fall into this trap. If that's not possible, check your stance in a mirror from time to time. Keep that head straight and upright. Don't let your cheek crawl forward on the stock or allow your neck to bend at an awkward angle.

Once you're hitting small targets consistently and at varying distances with the BB gun, it's time to move up to the real thing. Take your shotgun, along with a supply of ammunition and some clay targets, to an open field where it's safe to shoot. Place several targets upright on the ground from 10 to 25 yards away, and go through the same drill you practiced with the BB gun.

Shoot at each target quickly, without reference to barrel or front bead. Be

Using a BB gun without sights to practice hitting a ping pong ball or other small target is excellent practice. Remember to concentrate on what you're shooting at. Let instinct work for you.

Make sure your head is always properly positioned on the stock. Keep the head straight and upright; don't "crawl" your cheek forward on the stock.

Clay targets can simulate the flight of game birds, while trap and skeet shooting can expose you to all sorts of shots and the fun of competition as well.

sure you wear adequate ear protection so the muzzle blast doesn't throw you off stride. Lean well into the gun, and allow your body to move with the recoil. You needn't expend many rounds in this practice; it's primarily to acquaint (or reacquaint) you with the heavier jolt and feel of a real firearm.

The next step is to shoot at moving targets. You'll need a partner equipped with a hand trap for this. Before you begin to shoot, throw the gun to your shoulder a few times. Check your stance. Is your head in the proper position behind the gun? Does your body feel comfortably balanced? Are you bending forward slightly from the waist?

Practice swinging the shotgun to one side, then the other. Follow an imaginary target in flight. Are you moving your whole body, or simply moving the gun with your arms? Snap the trigger on an empty chamber while you continue to track the make-believe target. Did you stop your swing? The gun should continue moving smoothly without interruption, even after the trigger is pulled. Have your helper critique you on this. If he spots any stiffness or hesitation, make sure he points it out. Stopping the swing is a sure way to miss.

Have your companion stand behind you and a little to one side, and let him throw a couple of slow-moving clay birds across your field of view. Track these birds with an empty gun, moving the muzzle fast enough to catch up to and pass the bird. As your eye (which is the shotgun sight, remember?) moves past the target, pull the trigger. Again, have your coach watch carefully to make sure you don't flinch or halt your swing.

Put your ear protectors on and try the same thing again with the gun loaded. Stay loose, and let your instincts work—those same instincts you learned with the sightless BB gun will break moving clays almost as easily as they helped you hit paper cups and ping pong balls. Once the gun "shoots where you look," the rest is easy. Further improvement is simply a matter of additional practice and experience.

Clay targets can be thrown from a hand trap at varying speeds and directions to simulate the flight of different gamebirds. Trap and skeet shooting is also invaluable practice. Before long, you'll discover how to hit each kind of target. Again, let your instincts work for you. Don't consciously think about the amount of lead necessary to hit fast crossing shots or high, slow "floaters." Scientific analysis will do more harm than good here. After you've missed targets at certain angles and speeds a few times, your instincts will take care of the necessary adjustments. Trust them.

Much has been written about "swing through" and sustained leads, as well as "point and shoot" shotgunning for game. Consciously attempting to use any carefully prescribed system of leading a target has an inhibiting, often disastrous effect on your natural gunning instincts. My advice is to ignore such

You don't need a fancy, expensive regulation setup to enjoy busting clay birds. A friend with a hand-trap provides plenty of action and variety of target angles.

When your gun "points where you look," you'll be able to hit flying targets consistently. Be sure to use ear protection for practice sessions.

systems, and rely instead on your cerebral computer to get the job done. You might miss a slow-flying goose a few times, or strike out on fast-flushing quail. Remember, you missed those ping pong balls, too, when you first started shooting at them.

Concentrate on the basics: proper head and eye position, a natural, easy-moving stance, and smooth follow through. Keep that muzzle swinging well after you've pulled the trigger. Concentrate on the *target*, not the gun. Once you've developed the proper shooting instincts, they'll do the rest.

Try to stay relaxed. If you tense up, your natural shooting rhythms will be disturbed. If you miss a target, forget it. Your brain will be analyzing every miss, and storing up the data. Soon misses will become increasingly rare. If you *do* fall into a shooting slump, it can be very helpful to have another experienced wing shot stand behind you as you practice. Under the right lighting conditions, the shot string is visible as it travels to the target. An overcast day is best, and the observer must be standing directly behind the gunner. Your companion may be able to tell better than you can if you're shooting high, low, or behind the target. That kind of information can aid your instincts in making the necessary adjustments.

As your confidence builds, your score will continue to improve. Enjoy yourself, and keep practicing. It won't happen overnight, but one day you'll be shooting like an expert.

CHAPTER 18

Choosing the Right Shotgun and Load

In the preceding chapter I noted that the shooter's eye serves as the shotgun sight. I also stressed that the head must be properly positioned behind the gun, with the eye at just the right height. I made the point that the head should be reasonably straight and erect, and not craned uncomfortably to meet the stock.

Unfortunately, all these criteria can be thoroughly met only if the stock has the proper dimensions. If the buttstock's comb is too high and the shooter can see too much barrel, the gun will shoot high. Shotguns intended for the rising targets encountered in trapshooting are intentionally stocked this way. In effect, it provides the trapshooter with a certain amount of built-in lead.

Guns intended for hunting or the skeet range have a lower comb. Because shooters don't come with uniform facial features, the same stock will fit each gunner differently. A long, narrow face with high cheekbones will position the eye differently behind the gun than will a broad skull structure.

Shooter's arms also vary markedly in length. Very tall sportsmen typically have much longer arms than short gunners do. Other physical variations also come into play.

The majority of shotguns sold in American sporting goods stores carry stock dimensions that are more or less standardized. Lay the gun upside down on a table top (with the muzzle projecting so the front sight bead doesn't interfere), and measure the distance from the table top to the forward part of the comb. This gives you the amount of drop at the comb. Take a similar measurement at the butt end of the comb; this is the drop at the heel. The distance from the trigger to the midpoint of the buttplate or rear surface of the recoil pad is called the length of pull. Most American shotguns made for hunting will drop 1½ inches at the comb, 2½ inches at the heel, and have a length of pull somewhere around 14 inches. Those measurements will vary a bit from model to model, but not by much.

American gunners adapt surprisingly well to most factory-issue shotgun stocks. Most truly good gunners—those who regularly shoot competitively against other top marksmen—make their own alterations to improve the way standard stocks fit. A smaller number expend the time and money needed to have their stocks custom made.

There are a number of inexpensive adjustments any sportsman can make. If a stock is too long, he can have it cut down. If it's too short, he can increase the

Shotgun-stock length can be changed by either cutting a section from the butt end or adding a recoil pad.

length by having a recoil pad installed. Such pads come in various widths, and you can usually find a size that pleases you.

If you cheek the stock too low, you can build up the comb with layers of stick-on moleskin or other material. Any well-equipped gun store should have inexpensive kits on hand designed for this purpose. Take care not to add too much material at a time. Build up the thickness with several thin layers, testing the fit after each addition.

If the comb is too high, wood can be removed with rasp and sandpaper until it's the right height. This is a job that should be left to a gunsmith unless you're handy with woodworking tools. A common mistake is to remove too much wood, leaving the comb too low. The fit should be checked periodically as you work. When the stock feels right, you'll need to fine sand and steel wool the freshly worked wood. Then fill the pores with a good wood filler, stain to match the surrounding wood, and refinish with an aerosol can of epoxy or some other appropriate fininshing material.

While you may be able to shoot respectably with a gun that fails to fit you right, you can't help but do better with a stock that's correctly proportioned. The way the gun fits you is of much greater importance than gauge or action type.

You may not be able to afford a custom-made stock, but you can turn the small differences in standard stock dimensions to your advantage when you buy a new shotgun. When you've narrowed down your choices to several different guns, place them on the counter before you. Pick each gun up and handle it in turn. Close your eyes and throw the gun to your shoulder, then open them and note how much (or how little) barrel or rib you can see. Remember, if you see too much of the barrel's length when holding the gun in natural shooting position the gun will shoot high. If you can see only the tip of the front bead, it's sure to shoot low.

How does the comb feel against your face? Is it too narrow? Too broad? Does it ridge uncomfortably against your face? How about length? Do you feel like either arm is "reaching" as you hold the gun to your shoulder? Does the buttplate or pad catch on your upper chest or clothing as you throw the gun up? Does the gun balance naturally or feel a bit awkward in your hands? Try swinging the gun on an imaginary flying target. Does it move surely and smoothly? Does your eye maintain its position behind the barrel? Pick out a distant object, fix your eyes on it, and throw the gun up into shooting position. Only then look down at the barrel. Is it pointed directly at the target, and not too high or low?

Fitting a shotgun is a little bit like fitting a pair of shoes. The salesman (or fitter) can help narrow the choices, but in the final analysis you're the best

When buying a new shotgun, check the fit carefully. Look for feel against your
cheek as well as balance and swing. Pick a gun that feels right for you.

judge of what feels right. No one else can really tell what the gun feels like to
you. And you're the one who'll be using it.

After fit, the choice of choke constriction comes next in importance. What
kind of shooting will you be doing with the gun? If you'll be shooting trap or
pass shooting at high-flying waterfowl, a full choke may be right for you.
However, a modified choke will provide an effective pattern nearly as far and
is more forgiving at medium range (30 to 40 yards). It's a better choice for
most gunners.

For typical upland hunting, improved cylinder or even straight cylinder
(skeet) chokes will generally put more birds in the bag than a tighter modified
choke will. The improved cylinder is at its best from 20 to 30 yards, although it
will kill cleanly out to 35 yards and more. If you've been shooting a tight,
full-choked gun in the field, you'll be surprised how your marksmanship
improves if you'll give an improved cylinder gun a try.

Simply put, a more open choke throws a wider pattern and is therefore
more forgiving. You still have to be on target to kill cleanly, but a bird that's
not absolutely centered in the pattern won't escape. At close range (30 yards

and under), full-choked patterns are so tightly constricted they're likely to miss cleanly or badly mangle a bird. In effect, the modified choke represents some kind of compromise, but it's still primarily a long-range option.

Because the improved cylinder choke is so deadly at ranges from 20 to 35 yards, it should be the number one choice of upland hunters everywhere. It also works great for decoyed ducks. The vast majority of gamebird shooting opportunities come in that 20-to 35-yard range. The fact that more hunters don't take advantage of the improved cylinder's versatility can only be put down to ignorance. Tradition plays a part in this. If grandad used a full-choked gun that would "really reach out and gittem," your father likely made a similar choice. I chose a full-choked gun as my first shotgun through the same line of reasoning. When I finally made the switch to improved cylinder bird guns, my kill ratio instantly improved. Almost every really good wing shot I've known favored open-choked guns for most upland hunting—and that choice undoubtedly contributed to their superior marksmanship.

At one time, your choice of choke dictated barrel length. Full-choked barrels were 30 or 32 inches long, while modified tubes measured 28 inches. An improved cylinder-choked barrel was almost always 26 inches from muzzle to breech. That convention is still in place, but manufacturers like Remington now offer short barrels in a variety of choke constrictions. Barrel length is largely a matter of personal choice, although short barrels are faster handling and work well for close-flushing game. Longer barrels help smooth the swing. Contrary to popular opinion, a long-barreled shotgun doesn't shoot any "harder" than a short-barreled one. I once cut a 32-inch barrel down to 20 inches in 2-inch increments. There was no discernible velocity loss.

You can increase the versatility of any single-barreled shotgun by having an adjustable choke device installed. This allows you to tailor the choke constriction to the hunting conditions encountered. An increasing number of gunmakers now offer integral interchangeable choke tubes with certain models.

As far as shotgun gauge is concerned, the 12 bore is far and away the most practical choice for the vast majority of gunning chores. Trapshooters wouldn't thing of using anything else, and most bird hunters feel the same. The big 10 bore is useful only for hunting turkeys and high-flying geese; the few guns in this gauge are too heavy for easy carrying, and recoil mightily (except for Ithaca's autoloading Mag-10; it's heavy, but kicks no harder than many 12-gauge magnums).

Sixteen-gauge guns were once highly popular, but they've long since been eclipsed by lighter, handier 20-gauge scatterguns. A 20-gauge shotgun with 3-inch magnum chambers will perform nearly as well as a non-magnum 12. I like 20-gauge bird guns and use them often; they're lively and fast handling,

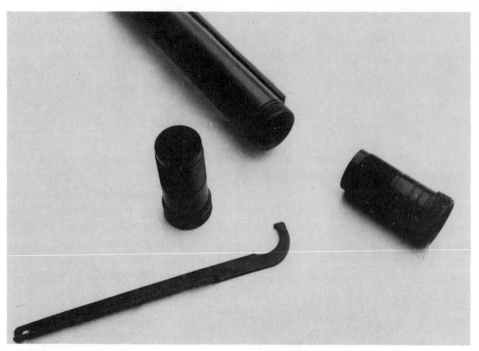

An increasing number of gunmakers now offer models with interchangeable choke tubes such as those shown here. This gives a shooter a great deal of flexibility at a nominal cost.

and can be deadly on game this side of the 40-yard mark. But the 12 is still more versatile. Smallbore 28-gauge and .410 shotguns are used in skeet competition, but are of limited use for hunting. A surprising number of .410's are used by hunters, but this gauge is the worst possible choice. The 28 is much more effective.

There are five basic action types available to shotgunners today: pump, autoloader, side-by-side double, over-under, and single shot. Each offers certain advantages and disadvantages, and each has its fans and detractors. The slide-action, or pump is a popular single-barrel repeater. It's relatively inexpensive, and most models are highly reliable. A good trombone-gun man can trigger repeat shots almost as fast as an autoloader shooter can get them away. Pumpguns are manually operated, and can be less fussy about their ammo diets than an autoloader might be. If you have a pump shotgun chambered for 3-inch shells, you can feed it everything from light 2¾-inch field and target loads to 3-inch magnum fodder without adjustment.

Autoloaders have the same, muzzle-heavy balance slide guns are noted for and may even be similar in appearance. Their primary advantage over

Manually operated pumpguns are highly popular in this country. This Remington Model 870 has a 26-inch barrel.

pump-action repeaters lies in the fact that their actions are cycled by gases of combustion bled from the bore at the moment of firing. This lengthens the time recoil forces react against the shoulder, modifying the sharp jolt produced by other action types into what amounts to a firm push. This results in less punishing recoil, which is an important factor to competitive target shooters who may fire a hundred or more shells in the course of an afternoon. Under these conditions, recoil has a cumulative effect that can spoil your concentration. Magnum-shooting waterfowlers also like selfloaders for the same reason: less apparent recoil.

If autoloaders have a disadvantage, it's the fact that most models won't digest the full range of target through magnum loads without some kind of adjustment. This isn't of serious consequence, as you're not likely to be firing both very light and very heavy loads on the same outing.

Double-barreled shotguns offer the advantage of making two different degrees of choke instantly available. They're also significantly shorter and may be faster handling than autoloaders or pumps. The reduction in overall length is due to the lack of a reciprocating action.

The choice between a traditional side-by-side double gun and a stackbarreled over-under is largely a matter of personal preference. The stackbarrel offers a narrower sighting plane that many shooters like, and is much more popular among American gunners.

Single shot guns are used by trapshooters as a matter of choice, and by other sportsmen as a simple matter of economy. A lightweight, budget-priced

Ithaca's Mag-10 autoloader tames the recoil of the heavy loads considerably and is popular with goose and turkey hunters.

Autoloading shotguns offer fast follow-up shots and reduced recoil.

single shot can kick unpleasantly with heavy loads, and if you miss the first time there's no second or third chance to redeem yourself. A few manufacturers still offer bolt-action shotguns. These are awkward, clumsy affairs that continue to sell solely because they're the least expensive repeaters on the market.

As I've said before, the way a gun fits and feels is vastly more important than the action type you choose. Action type is really a matter of personal taste and preference.

Buying shotgun ammunition is more complicated than simply selecting shells of the proper gauge. If your gun has a chamber 2¾ inches long, it won't

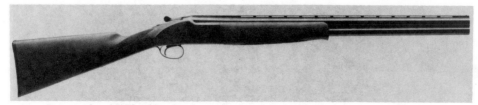

Over-under doubles like this Browning Citori Superlight are now more popular than side-by-side models among American gunners.

Single-shot, break-top shotguns are the choice of some budget-minded hunters . . .
as well as those who like to impose an additional challenge on themselves.

accept 3-inch magnums safely. Guns with 3-inch chambers will digest the full
range of loads in that gauge.

While there are standard-velocity target loads and high-velocity "Express"
and magnum loads for hunting, the most important difference is the amount
of shot each makes available. Actual velocity varies little between the different loads, but 12-gauge cartridges are available that throw as little as 1 and as
much as 2 full ounces of shot. Recoil varies with the shot charge.

The size of the shot is very important. Shot pellets vary from .05 to .33 inch
in diameter. Shot size is designated by number; as with fishhooks, the larger
the number, the smaller the object. Because shot charges are measured by
weight, you get more pellets per given load as pellet size decreases. There are
approximately 585 pellets in an ounce of No. 9 shot, and only 90 in an ounce of
2's. Thus shot size helps determine pattern density. The smaller the shot, the
more pellets your gun throws.

Clay target gunners like size 8 and 9 shot because fragile clays are easily
broken by the tiny pellets and the patterns are full and dense. Hunting grouse,
rabbits, pheasants, and other upland game generally requires 5's, 6's, or 7½'s,
while dove and quail hunters prefer 7½'s and 8's. Duck hunters like 4, 5, or 6
shot, while most goose gunners opt for 4's, 2's, or even BB-sized shot. Heavy-
bodied game requires the force and penetration only large pellets provide.

Steel (actually soft iron) shot pellets are required in some waterfowling
areas. Because this shot is less dense than lead, you should use one size larger
than you'd employ with standard loads. Steel shot also loses velocity and
momentum faster, so shots at extreme range should be avoided.

Traditional side-by-side double guns like this Fox Model B from Savage offer two
different degrees of choke and short overall length.

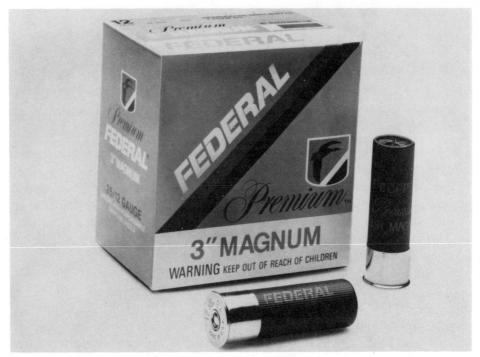

Three-inch magnum 12-gauge loads are now available with up to two full ounces
of shot.

For some reason, shotguns exhibit a marked performance for certain loads
and may behave raggedly with others. A gun that throws beautifully even
patterns with 1⅛ ounces of size 7½ shot may produce irregular, spotty spreads
with an ounce and a quarter of 6's. The only way to determine your own gun's
preferences is to pattern it with a variety of loads. To do this, tack a large piece
of butcher paper (available in most office supply stores) against a large
cardboard box or other disposable stand 40 yards (paces) away. Then fire,
aiming for the center of the paper. Using a 15-inch length of string as a
compass, draw a 30-inch circle around the heaviest concentration of shot.
Placing a thumbtack at one end of the string and tieing a broad-tipped
marking pen at the other makes this chore easy.

Next, count each individual pellet hole, daubing each with the marking pen
as you go. You can determine the approximate number of pellets in each load
from the following table.

Patterning your shotgun by shooting at butcher paper 40 yards away and then counting the number of holes in a 30-inch circle can reveal a lot about ammo. It's an exercise that's wise also for deer hunters in those states where shotguns are required.

Shot Size	Number of Pellets per Ounce
9	585
8	410
7½	350
6	225
5	170
4	135
2	90
BB	50

Next, divide the number of holes within the 30-inch circle by the number of pellets in the load. This will give you the pattern percentage. A full-choked gun should pattern between 65 and 75 percent at 40 yards. Improved modified patterns should average between 55 and 65 percent. Between 45 and 55 percent is modified choke performance, while an improved cylinder barrel should throw 35-45 percent spreads. A straight cylinder choke is supposed to deliver 25 to 35 percent patterns. You may be surprised to learn that your gun shoots tighter or looser patterns than the choke marking on the barrel indicates, particularly with certain loads.

How evenly is the shot distributed across the target? Are there gaping holes a bird could escape through? A gun that produces nice, even patterns with one load may yield splotchy shot clumps with another. This knowledge is important if you hope to get the best performance your scattergun is capable of delivering.

Patterning can also tell you whether your gun is shooting where you look. Make a small, but easily distinguishable mark on the target. Then walk 30 paces downrange, turn, rapidly mount the gun while you focus on the target, and fire. If the shot consistently patterns above, below, or to one side of the mark, your eye isn't in the right place behind the gun.

Choosing the right shotgun and load is important. To be an expert shot, you need a gun that fits you and feels right in your hands. It must shoot where you look. Unless the stock fits you properly, good instinctive gunning is difficult, if not impossible. The load must be one the gun likes and shoots well, and it must be appropriate to the game at hand.

CHAPTER 19

Skeet and Trapshooting

Trap and skeet are the target games shotgunners use to sharpen their skills, and can be an end in themselves. After all, you can shoot the breakable, saucer-shaped targets year-round and no hunting license is needed.

You needn't belong to a trap or skeet club to enjoy shooting clay targets. You can get excellent, low-cost practice with an inexpensive hand trap and a supply of targets. The person operating the hand trap should stand to one side or slightly behind the shooter and throw the targets either on command or unannounced. As long as both players have agreed on the rules, it can be both fun and instructive to try to take the shooter by surprise. Gamebirds don't fly on command, and this kind of practice more nearly simulates field conditions.

With a few minutes practice, a thrower should be able to present a challenging variety of target angles and speeds. Crossing, rising, or straightaway shots provide an interesting change of pace. If the shooter and the thrower trade places periodically, each can compete with the other. The thrower does his best to create difficult target paths, while the gunner tries to break as many clay birds as possible.

This kind of informal target practice can be a lot of fun, and it definitely helps your shooting skills. A lot of gunners use hand traps to brush up their

You can get excellent low-cost practice with an inexpensive hand-trap and a supply of targets. Look for sales, as prices of clay birds can vary depending on type and time of year.

reflexes each year just before hunting season begins. A better idea would be to keep in practice with periodic sessions throughout the year.

Trap and skeet shooting provides more formal competition. Meets are held locally as well as nationwide; this competition is supervised by the National Skeet Shooting Association and the Amateur Trapshooting Association. To find local trap and skeet clubs, check the Yellow Pages or ask around in area sporting goods stores.

Trapshooting originated in England sometime in the late 18th century, and was introduced in the United States around 1831. Live pigeons were originally used, but these have been replaced by the clay target that was invented in 1880.

A typical trapshooting layout consists of a concrete trap house set in front of five shooting lanes spaced 3 yards apart. The lanes are marked off in 1-yard

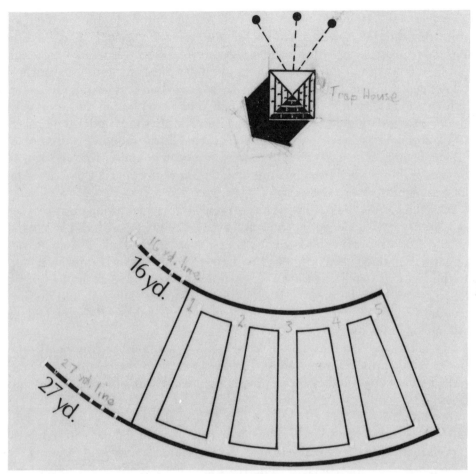

A typical trap-shooting layout shows the trap house 16 yards in front of the nearest shooting positions. Teams of five shooters can participate at a time, firing in turn.

increments, with the forward shooting station 16 yards behind the trap house. The rearmost station in each lane is 27 yards from the house.

Up to five shooters participate at a time, firing in turn. Five shots are fired from each position, then the shooters rotate by moving to the next station at the right. A total of 25 shots are fired in a full round of trap.

Trapshooters participate in three basic events. In the 16-yard event, all shooting is done from the 16-yard line in each lane. In the handicap event, each shooter is given a range handicap according to his ability. A beginner will shoot from 18 yards, while top experts fire from the 27-yard line. There's also a doubles event in which two targets are thrown at the same time. Single-shot trap guns may be used in the first two events, but a double-barreled or repeating shotgun is needed for shooting doubles. Because the clay birds in this game present fast-rising targets, most trapshooters use a gun with a high comb; this makes the gun shoot high, providing a measure of built-in lead and allowing the shooter to see the bird clearly over the barrel as he pulls the triger. With a standard field-stocked shotgun, you'd need to blot out the target with the muzzle as you shoot; otherwise you'd invariably shoot under the bird.

While smaller gauges are permitted, nearly all trapshooting is done with 12-gauge guns. The loads used in trapshooting can contain no more than 1⅛ ounces of shot pushed by a maximum of 3 dram-equivalents of powder. The largest permitted shot size is No. 7½.

The gun is mounted before the target is called for. A common mistake is for the shooter to first concentrate on getting the butt settled comfortably into the shoulder; he then cranes his head downward to meet the stock. This creates an unnatural, strained head position. The shooter should instead bring the gun up to the face and make sure the head is properly positioned behind the barrel. Then the butt can be brought back into the shoulder. There should be firm cheek-to-comb contact, but the neck muscles shouldn't be stretched or strained in any way.

To call for a bird, the shooter cries "pull" or some other command. The target should appear immediately. Targets are thrown at random angles, and must be between 8 and 12 feet high as they pass 10 yards in front of the trap house.

Because trap targets all fly away from the shooter, they require little horizontal lead—considerably less than for shooting skeet. Straightway targets require no horizontal lead at all. Again, the amount of lead required for each target angle must be determined by individual experience. This is where the instinctive form of shooting described in chapter 17 comes in handy.

Skeet shooting originated in this country around 1910, and the first national championship was held in 1927. Skeet more nearly approximates field hunting

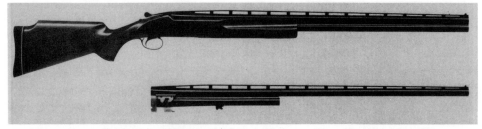

Guns made for trap shooting have a high, straight comb to elevate the face; this provides a built-in lead for rising targets.

A shooter breaks a target from the 27-yard line on the trap range. The ejected shell is visible immediately under the barrel.

conditions, and conventionally stocked shotguns are used. While trap guns are invariably tightly choked, very little choke constriction is used for skeet. Skeet also varies from trap in that four different gauges are used. Events are offered for 12, 20, 28, and .410-gauge shotguns, and serious competitors own matching guns in each gauge. Most beginners compete only in the 12-gauge matches until they feel ready for the additional challenge offered by the smaller-bored guns.

The skeet layout consists of seven separate shooting stations laid out in a shallow semicircle. A "high house" trap is located at the left terminus of the semicircle, and a separate "low house" trap is on the right end of the arc. An eighth shooting station is located midway along a straight line between the two trap houses. The "high house" at the left throws its targets from a height of 10 feet, while the "low house" at right throws from 3½ feet up. The targets emerge at the same angle each time, with the arcs set to cross at a height of 15 feet directly in front of station 8. Since the shooters fire from all points along the semicircle as well as from station 8, the angle of the target path in relation to the shooter is always changing.

Shooters fire twice from each station; once at a "high house" target, and once at a target from the "low house." "Doubles," or two targets thrown simultaneously from the two houses, are shot from stations 1, 2, 6, and 7. That uses up 24 shells. The 25th shell in the round—often referred to as the option

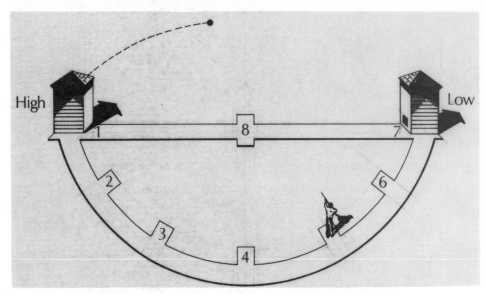

In skeet shooting, targets are thrown from a height of 10 feet from the high-house, at left, and from 3½ feet from the low house. Shooters fire from eight different positions.

A skeet shooter calls for a high-house bird. The low-house birds come from the skeet house in background.

shot—is used to repeat the first target missed. This target is repeated immediately after the miss, and must come from the same house. If you don't miss a target, you shoot your 25th shot at the end of the round at an extra target from any station in the field.

Because skeet targets move at a much sharper angle, a fair amount of lead is required, particularly from the center stations. The amount of lead needed at each station can be learned only through practice. Let your instincts go to work, and once your internal computer digests all the data you should start breaking targets with regularity. Shoot as soon as everything looks right; learn to trust your instincts. If you delay too long and try to follow the target with a sustained lead, chances are you'll miss. Make sure you don't stop your swing the second you pull the trigger; follow-through is important. Stopping the swing is one of the more common faults skeet shooters encounter, and it'll invariably cause you to shoot behind the target.

There are other kinds of competition practiced in this country, including live pigeon shoots. Live pigeons are popular targets internationally, and some matches are held in the South and Southwest part of the United States. But trap and skeet are the standard American shotgunning sports, and facilities for shooting can be found near almost any community.

Competing against others is important to a shotgunner's development, even if it's done only on an informal basis. Competition is fun, and helps you compare and evaluate your own shooting skills. Many shooters find skeet and trap so enjoyable they spend each weekend in practice or competition. This encourages a lot of shooting, and the more you shoot the better shot you'll become.

CHAPTER 20

Practice Shooting Skills at Home

Chapter 17 outlined a simple method for learning to shoot instinctively. It called for an inexpensive BB gun with no sights, and it could be practiced in your own back yard. This "sightless" method provides a highly effective means of learning basic shotgunning skills, but can be of similar value to riflemen. Rifles are carefully aimed instead of shot instinctively, but some hunting situations require fast shots at close, moving game. If you know how to shoot instinctively, hitting close, running game with a rifle becomes much easier.

Air rifles and pistols *with* sights also can be used at home in your yard. You need to make certain concessions to safety, like shooting only with a solid fence or some other large surface as a backstop, and making sure ricochets or bouncing pellets won't injure anyone. If you shoot an air rifle or BB gun at any hard, unyielding surface, the pellet can bounce back hard enough to cause injuries. Hardened shooting glasses or protective plastic lenses are recommended. Some pellet guns are potent enough for small game hunting and can be highly dangerous in careless hands. Whenever you're shooting a BB or pellet-firing gun of any kind, the Ten Commandments of Gun Safety should apply.

Air guns are inexpensive to own and operate, and they make almost no noise. Many models are highly accurate; formal air gun matches are popular in

Air rifles and handguns are quiet and accurate. They're ideal for home practice, both indoors and out.

many parts of Europe, and sophisticated match-grade pellet guns can be surprisingly costly. For casual practice at home, you don't need this kind of expensive precision.

You can shoot at small, paper bullseyes, ping pong balls, biodegradable candy wafers or just about anything that's cheap and disposable. The targets should be tiny enough to be challenging.

When I was growing up, I used to spend many summer hours shooting at flies as they would light on the back of our garage to rest in the heat. I all but wore out my Daisy air rifle shooting at the plentiful, pesky insects, and the garage wall was about worn through by the time I was old enough to hunt larger beasts. That was a long time ago, but I still shoot flies occasionally. It's wonderful practice, and it really hones your marksmanship skills.

You can even shoot an air gun safely in your home basement if you take a few precautions. Never shoot down a hall where another person could step into the line of fire unexpectedly. Always shoot against a blank wall with no windows or hanging pictures that could be damaged. A couple of large, cardboard boxes filled with old magazines and newspapers make an effective

BB guns, with or without sights, can provide excellent practice. There are quality
guns available in a variety of styles.

backstop for paper targets. Again, shooting against a hard wall can cause
pellets to bounce back toward you with enough force to do damage. Shooting
into magazine-filled boxes prevents this. Hanging old, cast-off blankets in
front of a wall also provides an effective, safe backstop.

With the right ammunition, you can even use centerfire handguns safely
indoors. Speer offers reuseable plastic indoor ammunition in sizes to fit .38
Special, .357 magnum and .44 revolvers, as well as for .45-caliber auto pistols.
Each cartridge consists of a hollow plastic case and a plastic bullet that fits
inside. No powder charge is used, and the plastic bullet is propelled by a large
pistol primer. The primer is seated in a small pocket in the base of the case,
and the plastic bullet is inserted at the front. The plastic projectile is fired with
enough force to cause injury if it strikes another person at a range of 75 feet,
but the bullet is easily stopped by the same kind of backstop used for airgun
pellets. Hanging blankets capture the plastic slugs effectively where they're
easy to retrieve.

Reusable plastic handgun cartridges, powered only by a primer, can be used in a home basement range. Make sure your setup is safe before you start.

Reloaders can manufacture their own indoor handgun ammo by using an expended cartridge case to cut soft bullets from blocks of paraffin wax. Again, these wax bullets should be powered only by a fresh primer; no powder should be used.

Dry firing can also be beneficial for rifle and handgun shooters. Before you start, make doubly sure the firearm is unloaded, with no cartridges in either magazine or firing chamber. Then make sure your intended target—a distant light switch, a spot on the wall, whatever—isn't located where an accidental discharge would cause injury or serious damage. We *know* that gun is unloaded, but you must still make sure you know where your bullet would go if it *was* to be fired. Inner walls are fairly thin and fragile, and a stray bullet can plow through several such partitions without much slowing down. If the rooms "downrange" are inhabited, pick another wall to practice your dry firing. Remember, treat every gun at all times as if it was loaded, even if you're totally sure it's not. That's how shooting accidents are prevented.

As its name implies, "dry firing" is simply the practice of squeezing off an imaginary shot while you hold the sights steady on some kind of target. It teaches good trigger and muscle control, and helps avoid the habit of flinching. If you observe the above safety precautions, it can be safely practiced indoors.

Regular practice at home is important. You won't always have the time to drive to the nearest firing range, but you can always step into the backyard for some fast shooting practice. BB guns and pellet pistols aren't a substitute for real firearms, but they require the same kind of skills. Using them regularly will help you shoot better.

CHAPTER 21

Safe, Show-Off Shooting Stunts

The primary satisfaction in becoming an expert shot lies in the confidence of knowing you can hit what you shoot at. This makes hunting more productive and enjoyable, and makes plinking and target sports a lot more fun. This confidence can also tempt you to show off your shooting skills occasionally.

While there's no real substitute for marksmanship, with a little of the right kind of showmanship you can look like a better shot than you really are. William F. Cody ("Buffalo Bill") and other turn-of-the-century entertainers often used shot-loaded cartridges in their handguns to augment their vaunted shooting skills. CCI/Speer and others offer both rimfire and centerfire ammunition loaded with quantities of tiny shot. These are available in .38 Special and .44 magnum handgun loads, as well as in .22 long rifle and .22 magnum rimfire cartridges for either rifles or handguns.

These cartridges aren't effective at long range, but at 15 to 20 feet they make gunning aerial targets relatively easy. Instead of needing to place a single bullet right on target, the spreading shot pattern produces a hit if you aim reasonably close. Too, the shot doesn't travel far, which increases the safety factor when you shoot targets in the air.

Penny balloons filled with water (be sure the necks are then tied) make inexpensive aerial targets that burst satisfyingly when struck by a single pellet. If you throw the balloons yourself, you can make the trick look more difficult

Shot-filled handgun cartridges can give your aerial shooting a boost. They also make shooting at airborne targets safer. It's a good way to impress friends with your marksmanship. It's up to you to announce the shells are actually the shot-filled variety.

(since you must throw, and only then aim and shoot). Actually, throwing your own targets can make them even easier to hit. If someone else does the throwing, you may get a crossing shot that requires leading the target; when you toss your own, you'll get a straightaway target that requires no lateral lead. As far as vertical lead is concerned, you'll need none if you'll only wait until the target is at the top of its arc. At that point it will appear to hang almost motionless for a split second; that's when to shoot.

Hitting thrown balloons with a handgun is both fun and impressive. If the spectators aren't aware you're using shot-filled cartridges, you can look like an expert with very little practice.

Actually, it isn't overwhelmingly difficult to learn to hit aerial targets with rifles or handguns using conventional ammunition. If you'll throw your own

Balloons filled with water burst for a good show when hit with even one pellet from a shotshell. You can look good and build confidence at the same time.

With a little practice, it's possible to hit thrown water-filled balloons or other aerial targets with a .22 rifle using conventional ammo. Shoot when the target is momentarily suspended at the top of its arc.

targets—which can be tin cans, overripe fruit, water-filled ballons, or just about anything that's handy and disposable—it doesn't take long to develop a controlled, underhand toss that allows the target to "hang" momentarily at the top of the arc, presenting a relatively easy mark. As always, you should know exactly where the bullet will go. A bullet fired at a sharp upward angle can travel a long way before it returns to earth.

You can learn the proper coordination with the sightless BB gun mentioned in chapter 17. Practice throwing a block of wood almost directly overhead, then shooting at it with the BB gun just before it begins its journey back to earth. Again, concentrate on the target, not the gun. With a little practice, you can learn the instincts required to consistently hit a properly thrown target.

An even more impressive trick that looks harder than it is is using a scope-sighted rifle to hit a target on the fly. For this stunt to work well, you need a riflescope with a wide field of view and not too much magnification. A 1½-4½X variable set at 1½X is ideal, although a fixed-power 4X scope isn't too much magnification if you're thoroughly familiar with both rifle and scope. Again, a straightaway target should be used, and you should pull the trigger the moment the crosshairs look right. If you can "hang" a rock or other target 20 or 30 feet above you, hold the crosshairs immediately under the target and pull the trigger just before the target starts earthward. While this can be done with a 4X scope, using a variable model set at 1½X provides a much larger field of view and doesn't much interfere with binocular vision. This means you can shoot with both eyes open, and that lets you find the target faster.

Once you're able to hit a flying target with some consistency using a centerfire rifle or handgun, there's a further refinement you can use to embellish your skills. Fill a 2-pound coffee can or some other tin container you can tightly seal with water. Place the lid on tightly. Next, place the sealed, water-filled can on level ground, atop a fencepost or on some other suitable surface. Place a smaller can directly on top of the liquid-filled container. Step back 15 or 20 paces, then quickly aim and fire at the center of the large, bottom can. A hit anywhere on this can will cause it to explode through hydrostatic pressure if the can was sealed tightly enough. At the very least, the top will pop off with some force. Either of these actions will cause the smaller can to fly skyward. Shoot that can out of the air (a fairly simple task if you wait until it's at the peak of its arc) and bystanders will be properly impressed. You need a reasonably potent centerfire rifle or handgun for this stunt; otherwise, sufficient hydrostatic pressure may not be produced. Once you get the timing right this trick is actually easy.

The plinker's favorite target is an empty tin or aluminum food or beverage can. Unfortunately, an empty aluminum beverage can is so light and offers so little resistance that .22 bullets often pass right through the can's walls without any other indication of a hit. You sometimes have to examine the can to make sure the bullet struck it.

It's much more satisfying—and impressive—when the cans bounce high in the air when hit. The trick here is to shoot not directly at the can itself. Instead, aim for the line formed by the junction of the can with the ground. If the bullet strikes the can right at ground level, the can will fly straight up for several feet. Actually, a hit slightly high or low will have similar results. If the bullet strikes the ground immediately in front of the can, the ricochet will throw the container backwards and up. If you're shooting a fast-firing .22 autoloader, it's no great feat to hit the can a second time while it's still airborne. Unfortunately, this repeat hit may or may not be apparent, depending on where the bullet strikes. As a rule, the can will jerk or twist in midair in response to a solid hit, as there's no ground-to-can friction to overcome.

Another fun stunt that can impress onlookers is to tie a water-filled balloon or a clay shotgun target to a length of string and hang it from a tree branch or some other support. If you use a clay pigeon, you'll first have to use an electric drill to bore a small hole in its edge to give you somewhere to fasten the string.

Cans can be made to jump impressively skyward. The trick is to shoot where the can meets the ground, not directly at the can itself.

Here's a great way to spend some shooting time. The trick to hitting this swinging target is to shoot when it's at either end of its swing.

Start the target swinging, then stand 20 or 25 paces distant and try to hit it.

Success is more a matter of timing than real marksmanship skill. If you'll carefully aim at either end of the arc the target describes, there will be a moment when the target hangs motionless in your sights. Shooting when the target is at the bottom of its arc is much more difficult, as it's moving at its fastest speed.

Another stunt exhibition marksmen are fond of is drawing some kind of a picture on a plain piece of paper with rimfire rifle bullets. This is a "connect the dots" kind of artistry. It's impressive, but requires fairly ordinary marksmanship skills. The most important point is to select an easily recognized image that can be produced without requiring a great deal of detail. Keep it simple. Then sketch the line drawing on a piece of paper, using a felt-tip marking pen to indicate the bullet strikes necessary to outline the picture. Try to keep the number of bullet holes required to a minimum. Then hang the target on a cardboard box or some other backing, and shoot for the indicated pen marks. After you've done this a few times you should have the bullet hole positions pretty well memorized. You should then be able to reproduce the picture on a blank sheet of paper. The beauty of this trick is that the bullet holes needn't be placed with super precision each time you demonstrate it. As long as the outline is reasonably recognizable the audience will be delighted. Keeping the range fairly short simplifies things—20 feet is good distance. This same stunt is harder with a .22 handgun, but it can be done.

Yet another show-off stunt that's easier than it looks is to snuff a candle flame with a rimfire rifle or handgun bullet without disturbing the candle. It's difficult to keep a candle lit outdoors, so you must offer some shelter from errant breezes by placing the candles in the open end of a roomy cardboard box set on its side. Don't place the candles too close together; make sure there's several inches between them. From a range of 20 to 30 feet, it's a fairly simple matter to snuff each candle's flame in turn. The truth is, you needn't center the flame to extinguish it; a bullet passing anywhere close creates enough air disturbance to do the job. Just make sure you don't shoot low and hit the candle.

Impressing onlookers with a shotgun is even easier. Instead of shooting clay targets thrown individually from a mechanical trap, try throwing two at a time into the air yourself and breaking them. If you'll use an open-choked gun, this trick really isn't very difficult. Hold the targets nested together and throw them high overhead in an underhand toss. The targets will separate as they climb, but will never be very far apart. If you throw them at a high enough angle no lead will be required. You can shoot them almost straight overhead, with very little gun movement required as you switch to the second bird. For

This trick is easier than it looks. Throw two nested clay targets skyward . . .

. . . and then break them both in mid-air (note the first target was dusted). If you use an open-choked gun and do the throwing yourself, it's easy.

someone who's learned to shoot fast and instinctively, this trick is duck soup. When you're breaking two targets regularly, try three at a time. Some exhibition gunners can break 5 or 6 targets before they reach the ground; *that* takes better gun handling skills and faster reflexes than most of us have.

If you'll use your imagination, there's no end to the shooting stunts you can perform. As your skills improve you can graduate to smaller, more difficult targets, and think of new ways to animate your plinking sessions.

CHAPTER 22

Firearm Care and Cleaning

Proper care and cleaning is needed to keep your rifle, handgun or shotgun performing well. A pitted bore can destroy rifle accuracy, and all firearms must be kept properly cleaned and lubricated to function reliably.

Rifle, handgun, and shotgun bores are cared for in pretty much the same way. Lead, copper, and powder residues should be removed after every shooting session; otherwise, moisture may collect in these materials and cause rusting and pitting of the bore's surface.

If at all possible, firearm bores should be cleaned from the breech end. Cleaning a rifle or handgun bore from the muzzle can damage the rifling in this critical area, and this can have an adverse effect on accuracy. Cleaning any firearm's bore by inserting a cleaning rod at the muzzle also results in powder residue, cleaning solvent, oil, and other foreign material falling into the action.

To do a proper cleaning job on firearms, you need a good cleaning rod of the proper diameter. Jointed rods are okay, but a stainless-steel or plastic-coated one-piece rod is best for rifles. The cleaning rod should come complete with jags to hold patches in place, and you also need one or more bronze brushes sized to tightly fit the bore. A supply of cloth cleaning patches and an oiled or silicone-impregnated cleaning cloth are necessary, and you'll need

Multi-purpose compounds can be used to both clean and lubricate guns. Follow the directions for best results.

both powder solvent and lubricating oil. Some products like Break Free and Marksman's Choice serve as combination cleaners, lubricants, and preservatives.

In addition, any complete gun-cleaning kit should include a supply of old toothbrushes, pipe cleaners, toothpicks, and other gadgets to help you reach those awkward nooks and crannies. A couple of screwdrivers sized to fit takedown screws also come in handy.

To clean a rifle, shotgun, or handgun bore, first soak a cloth patch in powder solvent (or solvent/lubricant combination), skewer it on an appropriately sized cleaning rod jag or tip and pass it through the bore. Place the barrel horizontally on a flat, level surface and allow it to set for 10 or 15 minutes to give the solvent a chance to work. Next, attach a bronze bristle brush to the rod and dip the brush in the solvent (never use the brush dry). Pass this brush completely through the bore several times to scrub loosened powder and lead deposits free. Finally, swab the bore dry with several clean cloth patches. If the last patch emerges nearly clean, you can follow this up with a lightly oiled patch to leave a preservative coating in place. If the last

Gun-cleaning kits are available from several manufacturers and most contain all the essentials you'll need for gun maintenance.

Here's a one-piece stainless-steel rifle rod and selection of cleaners and lubricants—choice items for a rifle-care kit.

Varmint shooters clean their bores after every 20 or 30 shots to maintain top
accuracy.

patch through is streaked with bright green or black stains, you should repeat
the entire process.

Target shooters, varmint hunters, and other riflemen who put a lot of
rounds through a smallbore centerfire rifle in the course of a day should run a
solvent-soaked patch, followed by a couple of dry patches through the rifle
bore periodically to maintain top accuracy and prevent the bore from leading
up. Many varmint shooters clean their bores every 20 or 30 shots, and some
target competitors do it even more often.

Rimfire rifle bores don't require such frequent care. Modern rimfire ammunition actually leaves a protective coating in the bore. As a matter of fact,
overly conscientious cleaning of a rimfire rifle bore can cause needless wear to
the rifling. Periodic cleaning is recommended, but you needn't scrub the bore
after each and every firing session.

Rifle, handgun, and shotgun actions should be kept clean of dirt and
powder residues. A toothbrush makes a very helpful tool for this work. The
action should be periodically disassembled for really thorough cleaning. After
cleaning, a *light* coating of lubricant should be left on the moving parts. Excess
oil attracts dirt and gums up the action.

Finally, wipe all exposed steel surfaces with a lightly oiled or silicone-

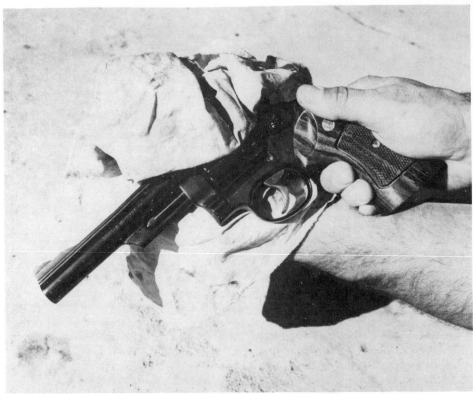

After cleaning, wipe all exposed steel surfaces with a lightly oiled or silicone-impregnated cloth before storage. The key word is "lightly."

impregnated cloth before you put the firearm away. This will prevent finger-prints from leaving unsightly rust marks, and should keep other types of corrosion at bay.

   If your firearm has become thoroughly wet in bad weather or through condensation (caused by bringing a very cold gun immediately into a warm room), you should disassemble it, dry it, and coat it very lightly with oil. Don't put this chore off, as rusting gets under way very quickly. Rust can be removed, but it's much easier (and less costly) to prevent its formation in the first place.

CHAPTER 23

Handloading Can Make You a Better Shot

Handloading can make you a better shot because you can get considerably more ammunition for your money. This means you can shoot more, and the more you shoot the better your marksmanship skills will become.

For shotgunners, the only reason to handload is the economy it affords. Factory shotshells are so good you're not likely to get better load performance by reloading. But you will be able to produce a lot more shells than you could otherwise afford. Few trap or skeet shooters would be financially able to stay in the game if it wasn't for reloaded ammunition. Competitive clay target gunners expend so many shells in practice and registered shoots that the ammo tab would be prohibitive for the average shooter. If you can afford to buy a case of shotgun ammo every few weeks, well and good. But if you intend to do a lot of claybird busting and your resources aren't unlimited, handloading can be your salvation.

Handgunners who make it to the expert ranks also burn a lot of powder, and centerfire handgun fodder is expensive. Again, handloading saves the day. If you scrounge castoff lead tire weights or other scrap lead and cast your own bullets, you can shoot extensively on a surprisingly small budget. Even if you buy all your components across the counter, reloading is vastly less costly than shooting factory ammunition.

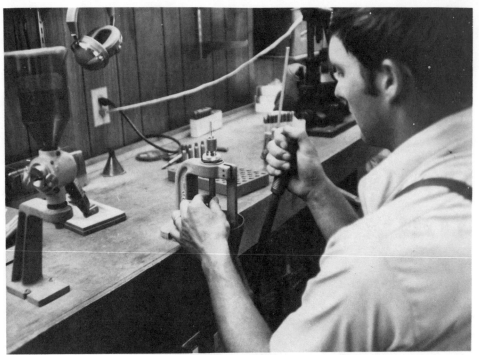

Handloading is easy, saves you money, and can produce superior ammo for your needs. Just be sure to follow the guidelines and recommendations supplied by manufacturers of the equipment and components.

Reloading riflemen can count their blessings two ways: they save money, and with a little careful effort they can actually make their rifles shoot better. By experimenting with different bullets and powder charges, it's possible to custom tailor a load for any rifle. Just be sure to follow recommended guidelines in handloading manuals. Factory centerfire factory loads are excellent, but a knowledgeable handloader can almost always improve on their performance.

Nearly all benchrest riflemen use handloads exclusively. The majority of serious rifle competitors handload their ammunition—not for the lower cost, but for the superior performance they gain. Many hunters reload primarily for the same reason: improved accuracy, and/or better performance on game. There is a vast array of centerfire bullets available to reloaders, while those who depend on factory loads exclusively have a more limited choice.

In short, you don't *have* to reload to become a better shot. But you're much more likely to achieve expert status if you do handload your own ammunition.

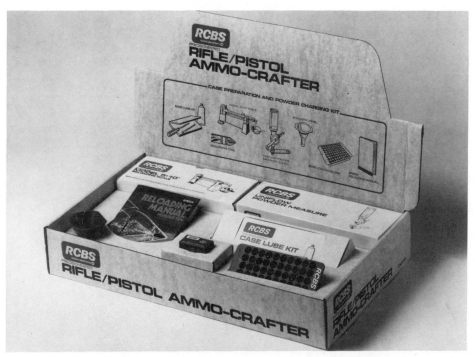

Complete reloading kits are available at reasonable prices, and the instructions are usually easy to follow.

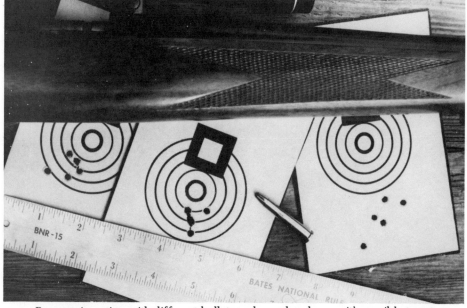

By experimenting with different bullets and powder charges, it's possible to get improved performance from almost any rifle.

Index